RAIL ATLAS GREAT BRITAIN & IRELAND

Compiled by **S.K. Baker**

Oxford Publishing Co.

A FOULIS-OPC RAILWAY Book

Sixth Edition
© 1990 S. K. Baker & Haynes Publishing Group
Drawn by: Thames Cartographic Services Ltd, Maidenhead, Berks.

Published by:
Haynes Publishing Group,
Sparkford, Near Yeovil, Somerset, BA22 7JJ.

Haynes Publications Inc.
861 Lawrence Drive, Newbury Park, California 91320, USA.

Printed by: J.H. Haynes & Co. Ltd.

British Library Cataloguing in Publication Data
Baker, S. K. (Stuart K.)
   Rail atlas Great Britain and Ireland – 6th. ed.
   1.   Great Britain. Railways. Maps, atlases
   I.   Title
   385.0941022

   ISBN 0-86093-474-8

GLOSSARY OF ABBREVIATIONS

ABM	Associated British Maltsters	L.L.	Low Level
ABP	Associated British Ports	LM	London Midland Region
AR	Anglia Region	LUL	London Underground Limited
ARC	Amey Roadstone Company	MDHC	Mersey Docks & Harbour Company
ASW	Allied Steel & Wire	M&EE	Mechanical and Electrical Engineer
B & I	British & Irish Line	MIFT	Manchester International Freight Terminal
BC	British Coal	MOD	Ministry of Defence
BICC	British Insulated Callenders Cables	MSC	Manchester Ship Canal
BIS	British Industrial Sand	NCL	National Carriers Limited
BOC	British Oxygen Company	NFD	National Fuel Distributors
BP	British Petroleum	NIR	Northern Ireland Railways
BR	British Rail	NSF	National Smokeless Fuels
BSC	British Steel Corporation	OLE	Overhead Line Equipment
BWB	British Waterways Board	PO	Post Office
C. & W.	Carriage and Wagon	P.S.	Power Station
Cal-Mac	Caledonian MacBrayne	PTE	Passenger Transport Executive
C.C.	County Council	P.W.	Permanent Way
CE	Civil Engineer	RHM	Rank Hovis McDougall
CEGB	Central Electricity Generating Board	RMC	Ready Mix Concrete (Marcon)
C.S.	Carriage Sidings	RPSI	Railway Preservation Society of Ireland
DCL	Distillers Company Limited	S. & T.	Signal & Telegragh
Dist	Distribution	SAI	Scottish Agricultural Industries
D.P.	Disposal Point	SC	Scottish Region
ECC	English China Clays	SGD	Scottish Grain Distillers
EMU	Electric Multiple Unit	SMD	Scottish Malt Distillers
ER	Eastern Region	SO	Southern Region
FLT	Freightliner Terminal	Term.	Terminal
GEC	General Electric Company	UES	United Engineering Steels
H.L.	High Level	UKAEA	United Kingdom Atomic Energy Authority
ICI	Imperial Chemical Industries	UKF	United Kingdom Fertilisers (Kemira)
IE	Iarnrod Eireann (Irish Rail)	WR	Western Region
LIFT	London International Freight Terminal		

PREFACE TO FIRST EDITION

The inspiration for this atlas was two-fold; firstly a feeling of total bewilderment by 'Llans' and 'Abers' on first visiting South Wales four years ago, and secondly a wall railway map drawn by a friend, Martin Bairstow. Since then, at university, there has been steady progress in drawing the rail network throughout Great Britain. The author feels sure that this atlas as it has finally evolved will be useful to all with an interest in railways, whether professional or enthusiast. The emphasis is on the current network since it is felt that this information is not published elsewhere.

Throughout, the main aim has been to show clearly, using expanded sheets where necessary, the railways of this country, including the whole of London Transport and light railways. Passenger lines are distinguished by colour according to operating company and all freight-only lines are depicted in red. The criterion for a British Rail passenger line has been taken as at least one advertised passenger train per day in each direction. On passenger routes, to assist the traveller, single and multiple track sections, with crossing loops on single lines have been shown. Symbols are used to identify both major centres of rail freight, such as collieries and power stations, and railway installations such as locomotive depots and works. Secondary information, for example junction names and tunnels over 100 yards long, with lengths if over one mile has been shown.

The author would like to express his thanks to members of the Oxford University Railway Society and to Nigel Bird, Chris Hammond and Richard Warson in particular for help in compiling and correcting the maps. His cousin, Dr Tony McCann deserves special thanks for removing much of the tedium by computer sorting the index, as do Oxford City Libraries for providing excellent reference facilities.

June 1977

PREFACE TO SIXTH EDITION

This sixth edition of the Rail Atlas of Great Britain and Ireland is fully redrawn in a clearer style, revised and further expanded. Five additional map pages have been added to clarify the complex areas of Cardiff, Bristol and North West London and to increase the scale of the electrification map. New insets have been added to clarify the detail in the Swansea, Neath, Peterborough and Preston areas.

This edition includes the many changes in the rail system since the previous edition and the significant growth in proposals for new stations, services and expansion of the network.

The author would like to thank the many people who have contacted him to supply material for this new edition. Thanks are also due to his family for their patience and support.

Stuart K. Baker
York
March 1990

CONTENTS

Publisher's Note

Although situations are constantly changing on the railways of Britian every effort has been made by the author to ensure complete accuracy of the maps in the book at the time of going to press.

KEY TO ATLAS

		Surface	Tunnel	Tube
British Rail – Passenger Also Irish and Isle of Man Railways	Multiple Track			
	Single Track			
Municipal & Urban Railways (London Underground Ltd lines indicated by code)	Multiple Track	C	C	C
	Single Track	C	C	C
Preserved & Minor Passenger Railways (With name, and gauge where other than standard gauge)	Multiple Track			
	Single Track			
Freight only lines — (British Rail & Others)	No Single/ Multiple Distinction			

Advertised Passenger Station : Saltburn

Crossing Loop at Passenger Station : Newtown

Crossing Loop on Single Line : *Kincraig*

Unadvertised/Excursion Station : Ennis *

Major Power Signal boxes	PRESTON	B.R. Region Breaks	LM ER
Carriage Sidings	C.S.	Colliery (including opencast site)	▲
Freight Marshalling Yard		Power Station	△
Freightliner Terminal	FLT	Oil Refinery	●
Locomotive Depot/Stabling Point	■ BS	Oil Terminal	○
British Rail Engineering Ltd.	▨ BREL	Cement Works or Terminal	■
British Rail Maintenance Ltd.	▨ BRML	Quarry	□
Junction Names	Haughley Junc.	Other Freight Terminal	
Country Border	///////	County Boundary	

IV

DIAGRAM OF MAPS

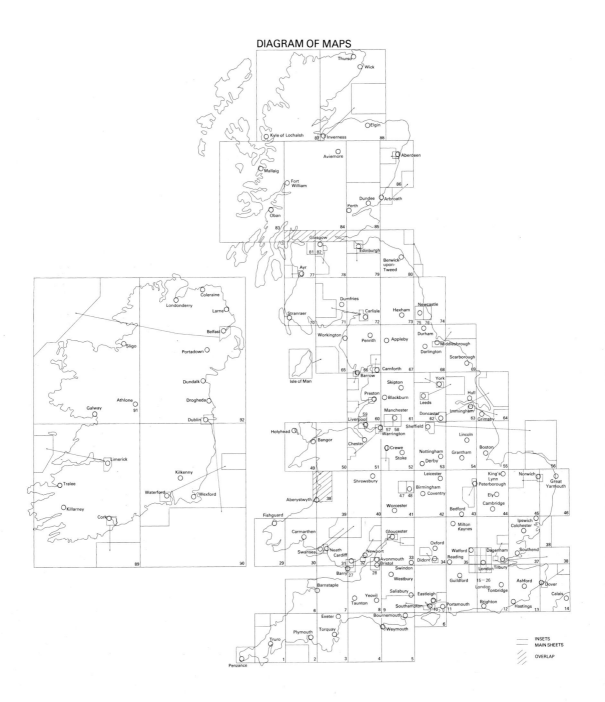

INSETS
MAIN SHEETS
OVERLAP

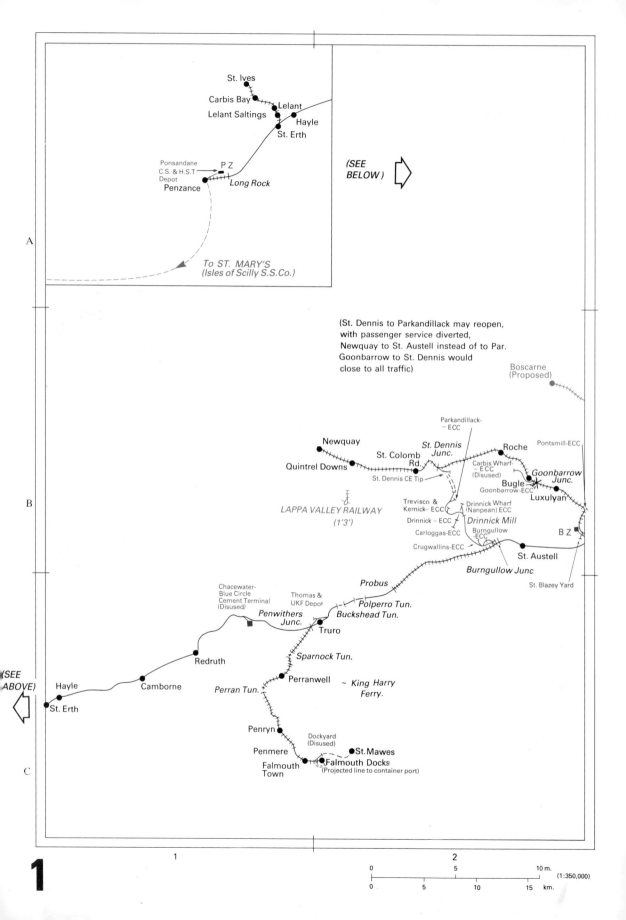

St. Ives
Carbis Bay
Lelant
Lelant Saltings
Hayle
St. Erth

Ponsandane
C.S. & H.S.T.
Depot
P Z
Long Rock
Penzance

(SEE BELOW)

A

To ST. MARY'S
(Isles of Scilly S.S.Co.)

(St. Dennis to Parkandillack may reopen,
with passenger service diverted,
Newquay to St. Austell instead of to Par.
Goonbarrow to St. Dennis would
close to all traffic)

Boscarne
(Proposed)

Parkandillack-
– ECC

Newquay
St. Colomb
Rd.
St. Dennis Junc.
Roche
Pontsmill-ECC

Quintrel Downs
St. Dennis CE Tip
Carbis Wharf-
– ECC
(Disused)
Goonbarrow
Junc.

Bugle
Goonbarrow-ECC
Luxulyan

LAPPA VALLEY RAILWAY
(1'3')

Trevisco &
Kernick- ECC
Drinnick Wharf
(Nanpean) ECC
Drinnick Mill

B
Drinnick – ECC
Carloggas-ECC
Burngullow
-ECC
B Z

Crugwallins-ECC
St. Austell

Burngullow Junc.
St. Blazey Yard

Probus
Polperro Tun.

Chacewater-
Blue Circle
Cement Terminal
(Disused)
Thomas &
UKF Depot
Buckshead Tun.
Penwithers
Junc.
Truro

Sparnock Tun.

Redruth

(SEE ABOVE)

Hayle
Camborne
Perranwell
~ *King Harry*
Ferry.

Perran Tun.
St. Erth

Penryn
Dockyard
(Disused)
St.Mawes

Penmere
Falmouth Docks
Falmouth
Town
(Projected line to container port)

C

1

1
2

0   5   10 m.

(1:350,000)

0   5   10   15   km.

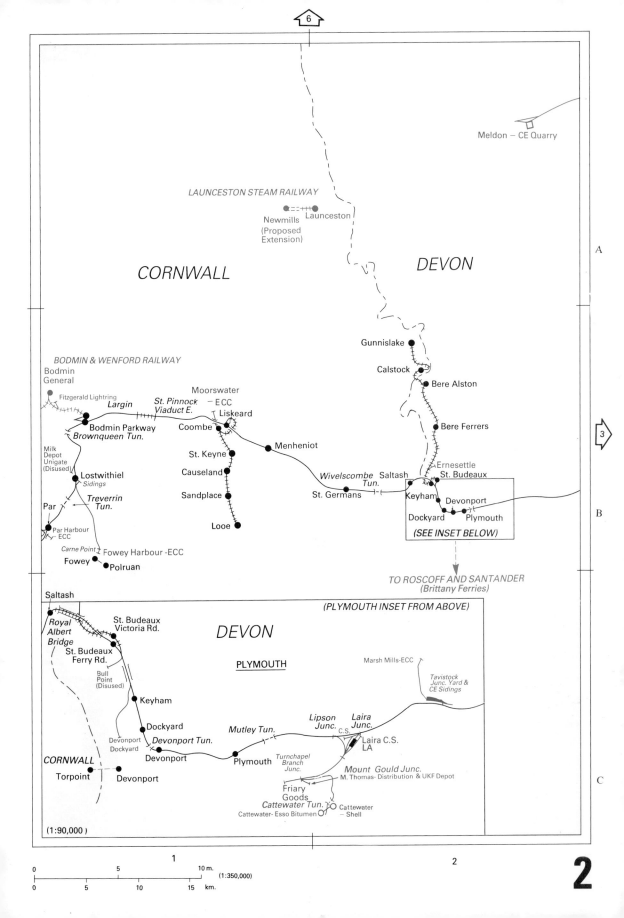

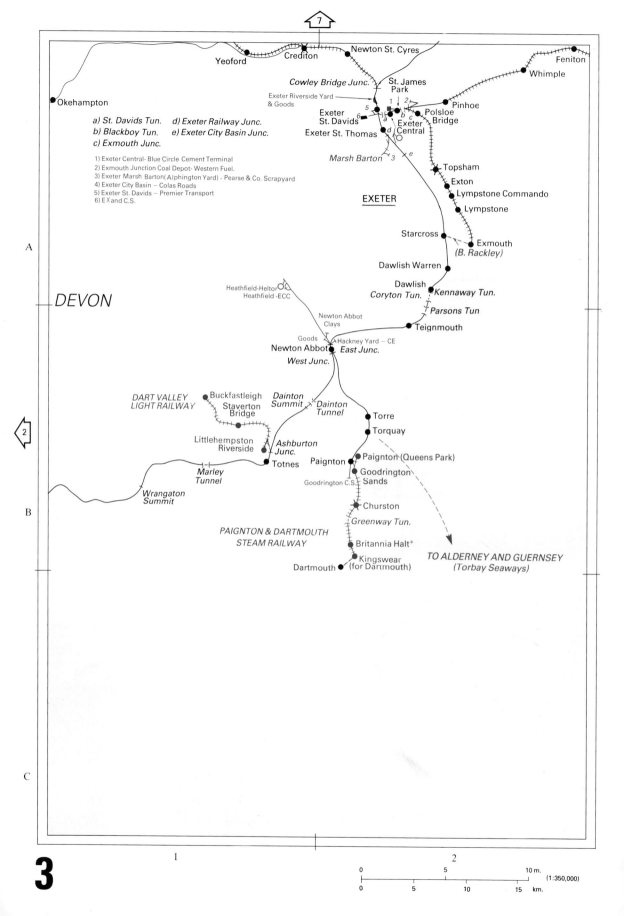

DEVON

Okehampton

Yeoford Crediton Newton St. Cyres Feniton Whimple

Cowley Bridge Junc. St. James Park Pinhoe

Exeter Riverside Yard & Goods Polsloe Bridge

Exeter St. Davids Exeter Central

Exeter St. Thomas

Marsh Barton

EXETER

a) St. Davids Tun.   d) Exeter Railway Junc.
b) Blackboy Tun.   e) Exeter City Basin Junc.
c) Exmouth Junc.

1) Exeter Central- Blue Circle Cement Terminal
2) Exmouth Junction Coal Depot- Western Fuel.
3) Exeter Marsh Barton(Alphington Yard) - Pearse & Co. Scrapyard
4) Exeter City Basin – Colas Roads
5) Exeter St. Davids – Premier Transport
6) E X and C.S.

Topsham

Exton

Lympstone Commando

Lympstone

Starcross Exmouth (B. Rackley)

Dawlish Warren

Dawlish Kennaway Tun.
Coryton Tun.

Parsons Tun

Heathfield-Heltor Teignmouth
Heathfield -ECC

Newton Abbot Clays

Goods Hackney Yard – CE
Newton Abbot East Junc.
West Junc.

DART VALLEY LIGHT RAILWAY

Buckfastleigh
Staverton Bridge

Dainton Summit
Dainton Tunnel

Torre
Torquay

Littlehempston Riverside Ashburton Junc.
Totnes Paignton Paignton (Queens Park)

Goodrington Sands
Goodrington C.S.

Marley Tunnel

Wrangaton Summit

Churston
Greenway Tun.

PAIGNTON & DARTMOUTH STEAM RAILWAY

Britannia Halt*

Kingswear (for Dartmouth)
Dartmouth

TO ALDERNEY AND GUERNSEY (Torbay Seaways)

0   5   10 m.
(1:350,000)
0   5   10   15   km.

3

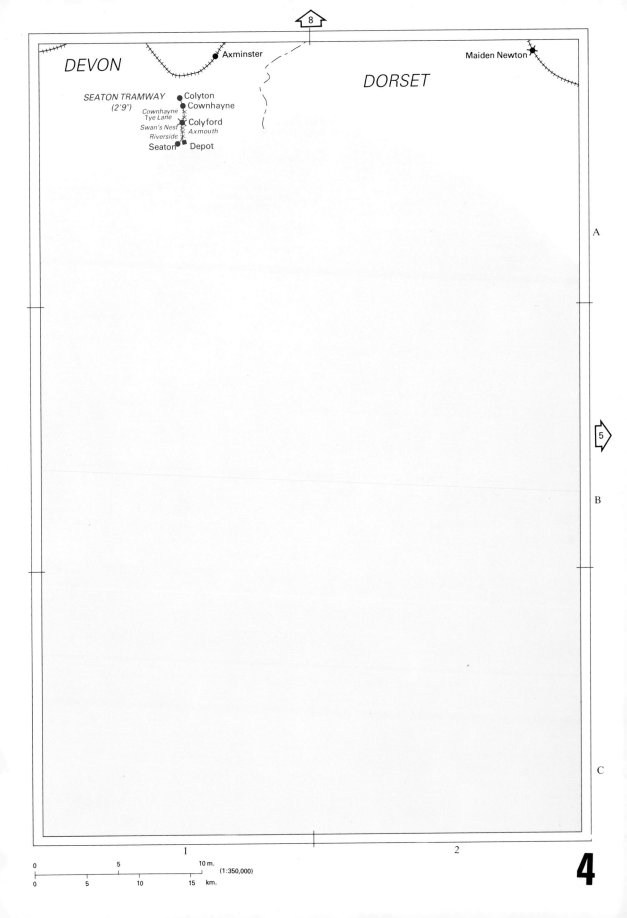

DEVON

DORSET

Axminster

Maiden Newton

SEATON TRAMWAY
(2'9")
Colyton
Cownhayne
Cownhayne
Tye Lane
Colyford
Swan's Nest   Axmouth
Riverside
Seaton   Depot

8

A

5

B

C

1   2

0   5   10 m.
                    (1:350,000)
0   5   10   15   km.

4

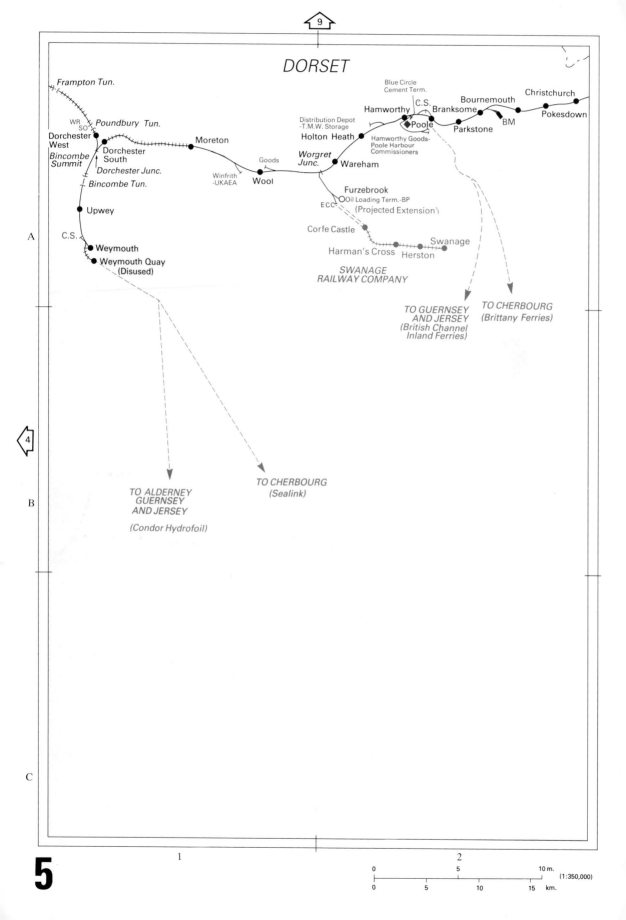

DORSET

Frampton Tun.

Poundbury Tun.

WR
SO

Dorchester
West

*Bincombe
Summit*

Dorchester
South

Dorchester Junc.

Bincombe Tun.

Upwey

C.S.

Weymouth

Weymouth Quay
(Disused)

Moreton

Winfrith
-UKAEA

Goods

Wool

Distribution Depot
-T.M.W. Storage

Holton Heath

*Worgret
Junc.*

Wareham

Hamworthy Goods-
Poole Harbour
Commissioners

Furzebrook

ECC

○Oil Loading Term.-BP
(Projected Extension)

Corfe Castle

Harman's Cross

Herston

Swanage

*SWANAGE
RAILWAY COMPANY*

Blue Circle
Cement Term.

Hamworthy

C.S.

◆Poole

Branksome

Parkstone

Bournemouth

BM

Christchurch

Pokesdown

*TO GUERNSEY
AND JERSEY*
(British Channel
Inland Ferries)

TO CHERBOURG
(Brittany Ferries)

*TO ALDERNEY
GUERNSEY
AND JERSEY*

(Condor Hydrofoil)

TO CHERBOURG
(Sealink)

A

B

C

5

1

2

0   5   10 m.

(1:350,000)

0   5   10   15   km.

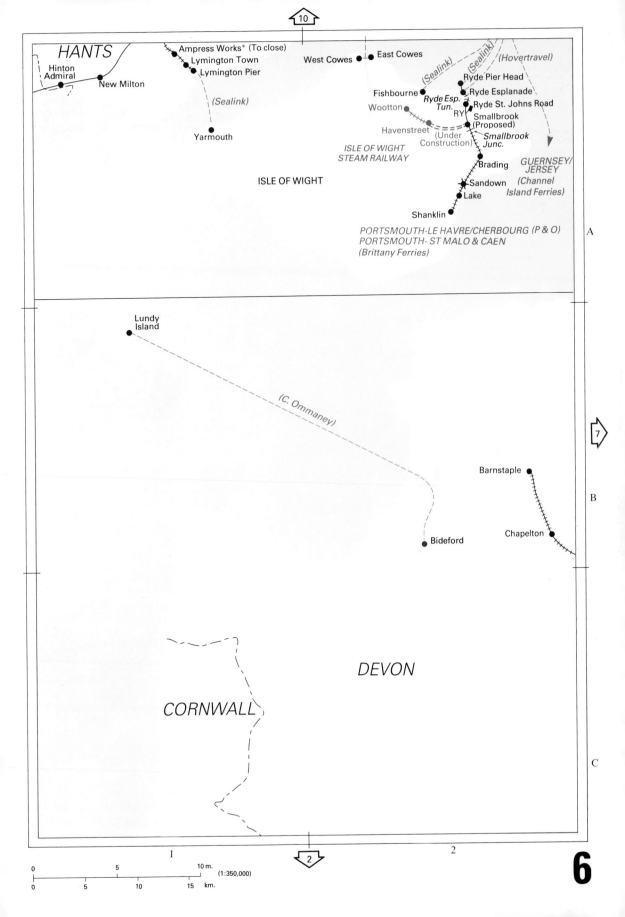

HANTS

Hinton Admiral

New Milton

Ampress Works* (To close)
Lymington Town
Lymington Pier

(Sealink)

Yarmouth

West Cowes   East Cowes

Fishbourne

Wootton

Havenstreet

Ryde Esp. Tun.

RY

(Sealink)   *(Sealink)*   *(Hovertravel)*

Ryde Pier Head

Ryde Esplanade

Ryde St. Johns Road

Smallbrook (Proposed)

Smallbrook Junc.

(Under Construction)

ISLE OF WIGHT STEAM RAILWAY

ISLE OF WIGHT

Brading

Sandown

Lake

Shanklin

GUERNSEY/ JERSEY
(Channel Island Ferries)

PORTSMOUTH-LE HAVRE/CHERBOURG (P & O)
PORTSMOUTH- ST MALO & CAEN
(Brittany Ferries)

A

Lundy Island

(C. Ommaney)

7

Barnstaple

Chapelton

B

Bideford

DEVON

CORNWALL

C

1

2

0   5   10 m.
|———————|———————| (1:350,000)
0   5   10   15 km.

6

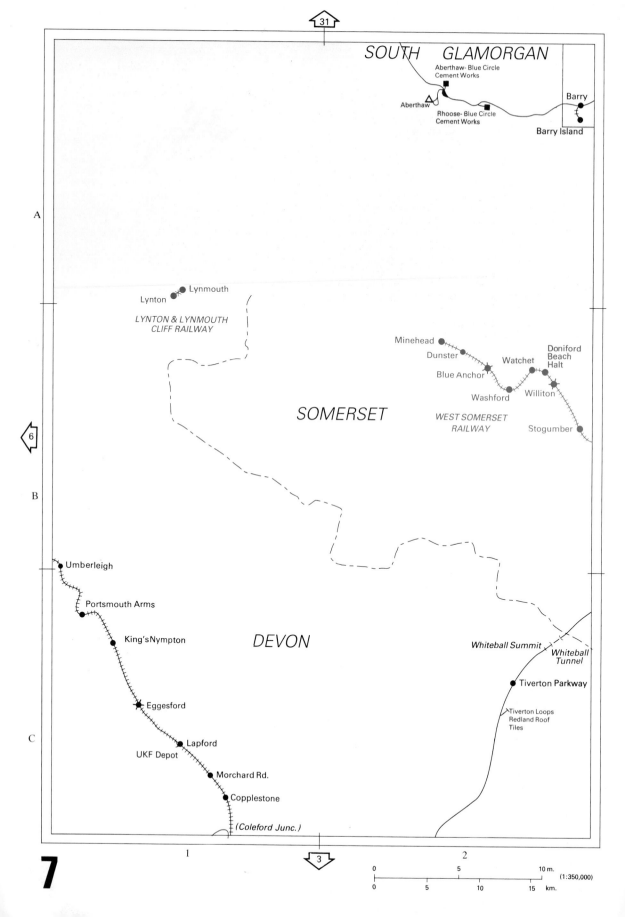

7

SOUTH GLAMORGAN

Aberthaw- Blue Circle
Cement Works

Aberthaw

Rhoose- Blue Circle
Cement Works

Barry

Barry Island

A

Lynmouth
Lynton

LYNTON & LYNMOUTH
CLIFF RAILWAY

Minehead
Dunster
Blue Anchor
Watchet
Doniford
Beach
Halt
Washford
Williton

SOMERSET

WEST SOMERSET
RAILWAY

Stogumber

6

B

Umberleigh

Portsmouth Arms

King's Nympton

DEVON

Whiteball Summit

Whiteball
Tunnel

Tiverton Parkway

Eggesford

Tiverton Loops
Redland Roof
Tiles

C

Lapford
UKF Depot

Morchard Rd.

Copplestone

(Coleford Junc.)

1

3

2

0   5   10 m.

(1:350,000)

0   5   10   15   km.

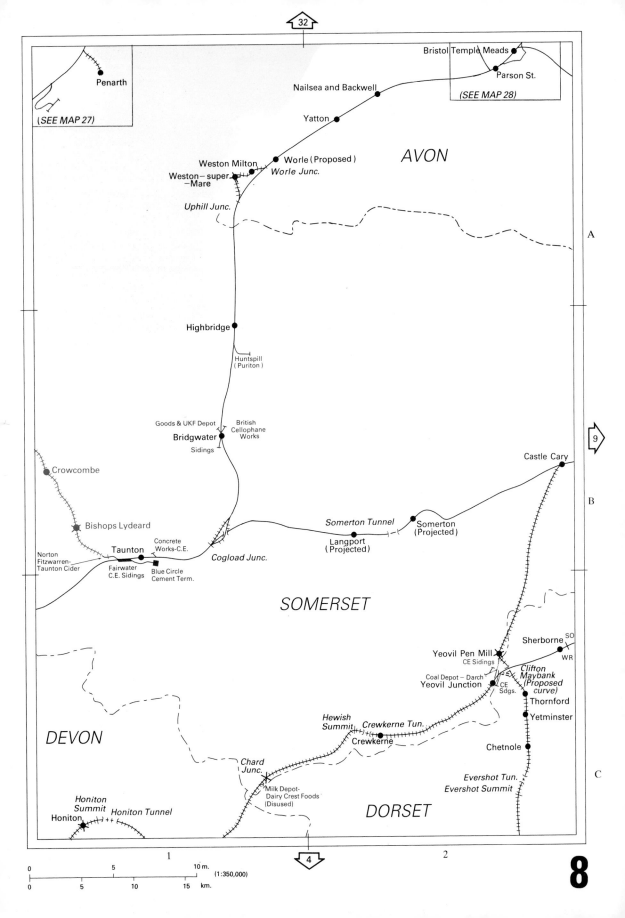

Bristol Temple Meads

Parson St.

(SEE MAP 28)

Nailsea and Backwell

Yatton

AVON

Worle (Proposed)

Weston Milton
Worle Junc.

Weston−super−Mare

Uphill Junc.

A

Highbridge

Huntspill (Puriton)

Penarth

(SEE MAP 27)

Goods & UKF Depot

Bridgwater

Sidings

British Cellophane Works

Castle Cary

9

Crowcombe

Bishops Lydeard

Somerton Tunnel

Somerton (Projected)

B

Langport (Projected)

Taunton

Concrete Works-C.E.

Norton Fitzwarren-Taunton Cider

Fairwater C.E. Sidings

Blue Circle Cement Term.

Cogload Junc.

SOMERSET

Sherborne
SO

Yeovil Pen Mill
CE Sidings
WR

Coal Depot − Darch

Yeovil Junction

CE Sdgs.

Clifton Maybank (Proposed curve)

Thornford

Yetminster

DEVON

Hewish Summit

Crewkerne Tun.

Crewkerne

Chetnole

Chard Junc.

Milk Depot- Dairy Crest Foods (Disused)

Evershot Tun.
Evershot Summit

C

Honiton Summit *Honiton Tunnel*

Honiton

DORSET

4

0   5   10 m.

(1:350,000)

0   5   10   15   km.

8

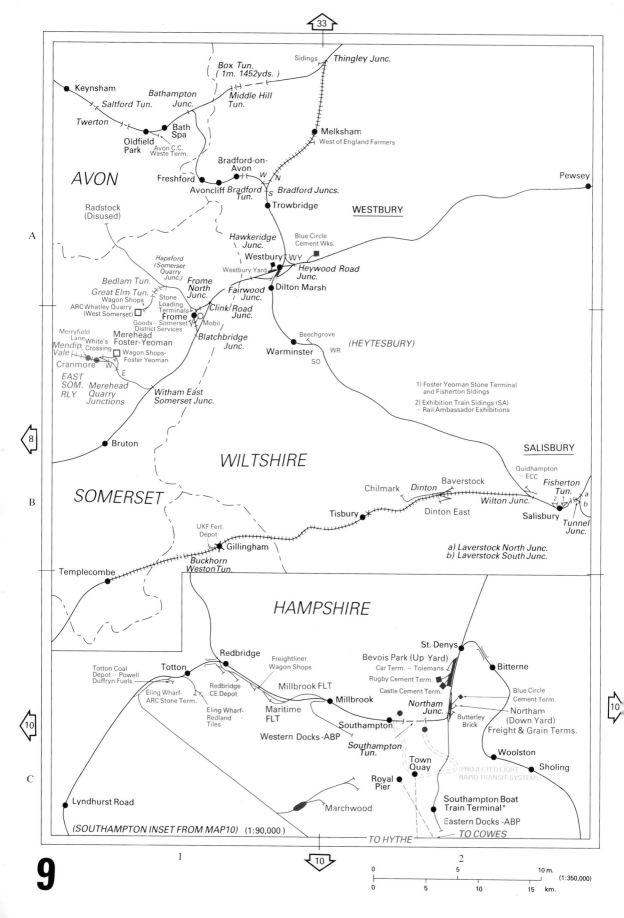

Keynsham

Saltford Tun.

Bathampton Junc.

Box Tun.
(1m. 1452yds.)

Middle Hill Tun.

Sidings

Thingley Junc.

Twerton

Oldfield Park

Bath Spa

Melksham

West of England Farmers

AVON

Freshford

Bradford-on-Avon

Pewsey

Avoncliff *Bradford Tun.*

W N

Bradford Juncs.

S

Trowbridge

WESTBURY

Radstock (Disused)

A

Hawkeridge Junc.

Blue Circle Cement Wks.

Bedlam Tun.

Great Elm Tun.

Wagon Shops

ARC Whatley Quarry (West Somerset)

Hapsford (Somerset Quarry Junc.)

Stone Loading Terminals

Westbury WY

Westbury Yard

Heywood Road Junc.

Frome North Junc.

Dilton Marsh

Fairwood Junc.

Goods – Somerset District Services

Clink Road Junc.

Frome

Mobil

(HEYTESBURY)

Merryfield Lane

Mendip Vale

White's Crossing

Merehead Foster-Yeoman

Wagon Shops – Foster Yeoman

Blatchbridge Junc.

Beechgrove

WR

Cranmore

W

E

EAST SOM. RLY

Merehead Quarry Junctions

Witham East Somerset Junc.

Warminster

SO

1) Foster Yeoman Stone Terminal and Fisherton Sidings

2) Exhibition Train Sidings (SA) – Rail Ambassador Exhibitions

Bruton

WILTSHIRE

SALISBURY

Quidhampton – ECC

8

SOMERSET

Chilmark

Dinton

Baverstock

Fisherton Tun.

2 1

a
b

B

Tisbury

Dinton East

Wilton Junc.

Salisbury

Tunnel Junc.

UKF Fert. Depot

a) Laverstock North Junc.

b) Laverstock South Junc.

Gillingham

Buckhorn Weston Tun.

Templecombe

HAMPSHIRE

St. Denys

Redbridge

Bevois Park (Up Yard)

Bitterne

Totton Coal Depot – Powell Duffryn Fuels

Totton

Freightliner Wagon Shops

Car Term. – Tolemans

Rugby Cement Term.

Redbridge CE Depot

Millbrook FLT

Castle Cement Term.

Blue Circle Cement Term.

Eling Wharf-ARC Stone Term.

Millbrook

Northam Junc.

Northam (Down Yard) Freight & Grain Terms.

Eling Wharf-Redland Tiles

Maritime FLT

Butterley Brick

Southampton

Western Docks -ABP

Woolston

Southampton Tun.

Sholing

C

Town Quay

(PROJECTED LIGHT RAPID TRANSIT SYSTEM)

Royal Pier

Lyndhurst Road

Marchwood

Southampton Boat Train Terminal*

Eastern Docks -ABP

TO HYTHE

TO COWES

(SOUTHAMPTON INSET FROM MAP10) (1:90,000)

10

9

1

10

2

0   5   10 m.

0   5   10   15   km.

(1:350,000)

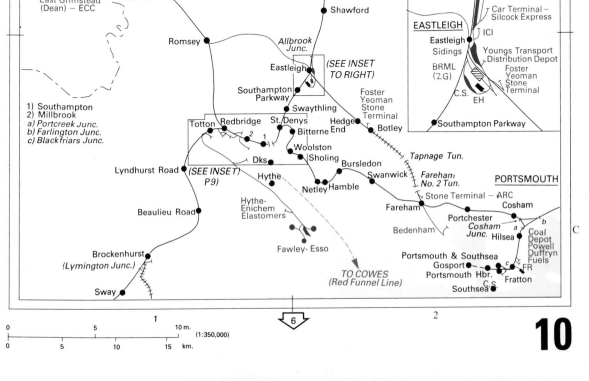

10

BERKSHIRE

HAMPSHIRE

Savernake Summit

Bedwyn
Hungerford
Kintbury
Newbury
Newbury Racecourse
BP
Thatcham
Midgham
Aldermaston
CE
Mortimer
Bramley

Blue Circle Cement Term.
Foster Yeoman Stone Term.
Murco
ARC Stone Term.
Theale
Conoco
Padworth – Goodwin
Coal Depot & Stone

Basingstoke
Sidings
Barton Mill C.S.
Bas. G.W.R. Junc.
Worting Junc.
BASINGSTOKE

Ludgershall*
Ludgershall (Tidworth)
UKF Depot
Andover
(Red Post Junc.)
Grateley

Whitchurch
Overton

Litchfield Tun.
Popham No.1 Tun.
Popham No. 2 Tun.
Elf
Amoc
Micheldever

Wallers Ash Tun.

MID-HANTS RAILWAY
Medstead
Alresford
Ropley

Winchester

Dean
East Grimstead (Dean) – ECC
Dean Hill
Mottisfont
Dunbridge
Shawford

Romsey
Allbrook Junc.
Eastleigh
(SEE INSET TO RIGHT)

Southampton Parkway
Swaythling

Foster Yeoman Stone Terminal

1) Southampton
2) Millbrook
a) Portcreek Junc.
b) Farlington Junc.
c) Blackfriars Junc.

Totton
Redbridge
St. Denys
Bitterne
Woolston
Sholing
Hedge End
Botley

Dks
Lyndhurst Road
(SEE INSET P9)
Hythe
Netley
Hamble
Bursledon
Swanwick
Tapnage Tun.
Fareham No. 2 Tun.

Beaulieu Road
Hythe-Enichem Elastomers
Fawley- Esso

Brockenhurst
(Lymington Junc.)

Sway

Stone Terminal – ARC
Fareham
Bedenham
Cosham Junc.
Cosham
Hilsea
Portchester
a
b
c
PORTSMOUTH
Coal Depot
Powell Duffryn Fuels

Portsmouth & Southsea
Gosport
Portsmouth Hbr.
Fratton
FR
C.S.
Southsea

TO COWES
(Red Funnel Line)

Inset: EASTLEIGH (1:90,000)

Allbrook Junc.
East Yard
Eastleigh CE Depot
Car Terminal – Silcock Express
ICI
Eastleigh Sidings
Youngs Transport Distribution Depot
Foster Yeoman Stone Terminal
BRML (ZG)
C.S.
EH
Southampton Parkway

A

B

C

34

6

11

0   5   1   10 m.
0   5   10   15 km.
(1:350,000)

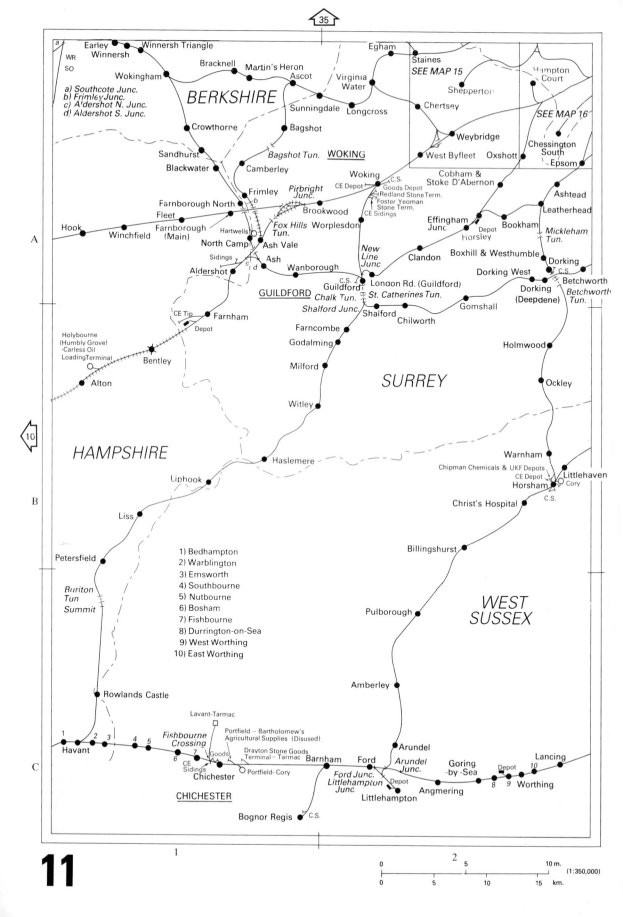

a
WR
SO

a) Southcote Junc.
b) Frimley Junc.
c) Aldershot N. Junc.
d) Aldershot S. Junc.

BERKSHIRE

Earley
Winnersh
Winnersh Triangle
Bracknell
Martin's Heron
Wokingham
Ascot
Virginia Water
Egham
Staines

SEE MAP 15

Hampton Court

Shepperton
Chertsey

SEE MAP 16

Sunningdale
Longcross
Crowthorne
Bagshot
Weybridge
West Byfleet
Oxshott
Chessington South
Epsom

Sandhurst
Bagshot Tun.
WOKING
Blackwater
Camberley
Woking
C.S.
Cobham & Stoke D'Abernon
Ashtead

Frimley
Pirbright Junc.
CE Depot
Goods Depot
Redland Stone Term.
Foster Yeoman Stone Term.
CE Sidings
Leatherhead

Farnborough North
Brookwood
Effingham Junc.
Bookham
Mickleham Tun.

Fleet
Fox Hills Tun.
Worplesdon
Horsley
Depot

Hook
Winchfield
Farnborough (Main)
Hartwells
Ash Vale
New Line Junc.
Clandon
Boxhill & Westhumble
Dorking

A
North Camp
Ash
Wanborough
Dorking West
Betchworth

Sidings
c
d
London Rd. (Guildford)
Dorking (Deepdene)
Betchworth Tun.

Aldershot
b
C.S.
Guildford
St. Catherines Tun.
Gomshall

GUILDFORD
Chalk Tun.
Shalford Junc.
Shalford
Chilworth

CE Tip
Farnham
Farncombe
Holmwood

Depot
Godalming
Ockley

Holybourne
(Humbly Grove)
-Carless Oil
Loading Terminal
Bentley
Milford
SURREY

Alton
Witley
Warnham

HAMPSHIRE
Haslemere
Chipman Chemicals & UKF Depots
CE Depot
Littlehaven
Cory

Liphook
Horsham
C.S.

10
Liss
Christ's Hospital

B
Petersfield
Billingshurst

1) Bedhampton
2) Warblington
3) Emsworth
4) Southbourne
5) Nutbourne
6) Bosham
7) Fishbourne
8) Durrington-on-Sea
9) West Worthing
10) East Worthing

WEST SUSSEX

Buriton Tun Summit
Pulborough

Amberley

Rowlands Castle

Lavant-Tarmac
Portfield – Bartholomew's
Agricultural Supplies (Disused)
Arundel

Fishbourne Crossing
Drayton Stone Goods
Terminal – Tarmac
Ford
Arundel Junc.
Goring-by-Sea
Lancing

1
2
3
4
5
7
Goods
Barnham
Depot
10
Depot

C
Havant
6
CE Sidings
Chichester
Portfield- Cory
Ford Junc.
Littlehampton Junc.
Depot
Angmering
8
9
Worthing

CHICHESTER
Littlehampton

Bognor Regis
C.S.

11

1
2
0   5   10 m.
(1:350,000)
0   5   10   15 km.

Wimbledon
West Croydon
SEE MAP 17
Addiscombe
East Croydon
Hayes
Bromley N.
St. Mary Cray
Bickley
Petts Wood
ON
Orpington
Chelsfield
Chelsfield Tun.
Knockholt
Swanley
Farningham Road
Longfield
Eynsford Tun.
Eynsford
Meopham
Sole
North Downs Tun.
Strood Tun.
(1m. 569 yds.)
Cuxton
Halling Rugby Cem. Wks.
Shoreham
Otford
(Projected Railway Approximate Route)
Halling
Snodland
New Hythe
Brookgate – Reed Paper
Aylesford

GREATER LONDON
SEE MAP 18

Sutton
Purley
Riddlesdown
Upper Warlingham
Banstead
Reedham
Epsom Downs
Kingswood Tun.
Tadworth
Coulsdon South
Caterham
Woldingham
Oxted Tun. (1m. 501 yds.)

KENT

Otford
Kemsing
Dunton Green
Bat & Ball
Sevenoaks
C.S.
Sevenoaks Tun. (1m. 1693 yds.)
Borough Green & Wrotham
West Malling
East Malling
Wateringbury
Yalding
A

Merstham Old Tun. (1m. 71yds.)
Quarry Tun. (1m. 353 yds.)
Merstham
Redhill
C.S.
Reigate
C.S.
Hydleman
Earlswood
Nutfield
Holmethorpe – British Ind. Sand
Redhill Tun.
Bletchingley Tun.
Godstone
CE Tip
Oxted
Hurst Green
OXTED
Limpsfield Tun.
Hurst Green Junc.
Edenbridge Tun.
Edenbridge
Edenbridge Town
Hever
Penshurst
Leigh
Hildenborough
East Peckham CE Tip
Tonbridge
West Yard C.S.
Somerhill Tun.
Philips & Whirlpool
Paddock Wood
Beltring

Salfords
Brett Marine Stone Terminal
Q8 Petroleum (Proposed)
Horley
RMC Sand Terminal
C.S.
Foster Yeoman Stone Terminal
Dor to Dor
North Terminal Peoplemover
Gatwick Airport
Crawley New Yard
THREE BRIDGES
Three Bridges
Sidings
Three Bridges CE Depot
Ifield
Crawley
Faygate
Balcombe Tun.
Sharpthorne Tun.
Lingfield
Dormans
East Grinstead
Kingscote
(UNDER CONSTRUCTION)
West Hoathly
BLUEBELL RAILWAY
Horsted Keynes
Sidings
Mark Beech Tun.
Cowden
Blackham
Ashurst
Eridge
Crowborough
Crowborough Tun.
Tunbridge Wells
Wells Tun.
Grove Hill Tun.
Strawberry Hill Tun.
Frant
High Brooms
Cory
Wadhurst
Wadhurst Tun.
Stonegate
Etchingham
B

Balcombe
Ardingly ARC Stone Terminal
Copyhold Junc.
Haywards Heath
Haywards Heath Tun.
Ketches Farm Halt
Sheffield Park
Greenhurst
Buxted
Uckfield

1) Smitham
2) Woodmansterne
3) Chipstead
4) Whyteleafe South
5) Kenley
6) Whyteleafe
7) Kingswood
8) Tattenham Corner
9) Southwick
10) Fishersgate
11) Portslade
12) Aldrington
a) Cliftonville Tunnel
b) Hove Tunnel
c) Stoats Nest Junc.

Mountfield – British Gypsum

Wivelsfield
Keymer Junc.
Burgess Hill
Hassocks
LAVENDER LINE
Dingley Dell
Plumpton
Isfield
Cooksbridge
(PROJECTED RAILWAY)

EAST SUSSEX

Clayton Tun. (1m. 499 yds.)
Kingston Tun.
Lewes Tun.
Falmer Tun.
Patcham Tun.
Preston Park
C.S. & Coal Depot - Powell Duffryn
C.S.
BI
Falmer
Southerham Junc.
Moulsecoomb
London Road (Brighton)
Montpelier Junc.
Southease
Glynde
Berwick
Polegate
Normans Bay
Pevensey
Collington
Cooden Beach
Pevensey & Westham
C

Shoreham -by-Sea
9 10 11 12
Hove
Brighton
Aquarium
Marina
Peter Pan's Playground & Depot
VOLK'S ELECTRIC RLY. (2'8½")
Newhaven Town
Newhaven Harbour
Newhaven Marine
Bishopstone
James Fisher
Seaford
TO DIEPPE (Sealink)
Aggregate Loading Term. – RMC
Willingdon Junc.
Hampden Park
C.S.
Eastbourne

0   5   10 m.
0   5   10   15 km.
(1:350,000)

1   2

12

13

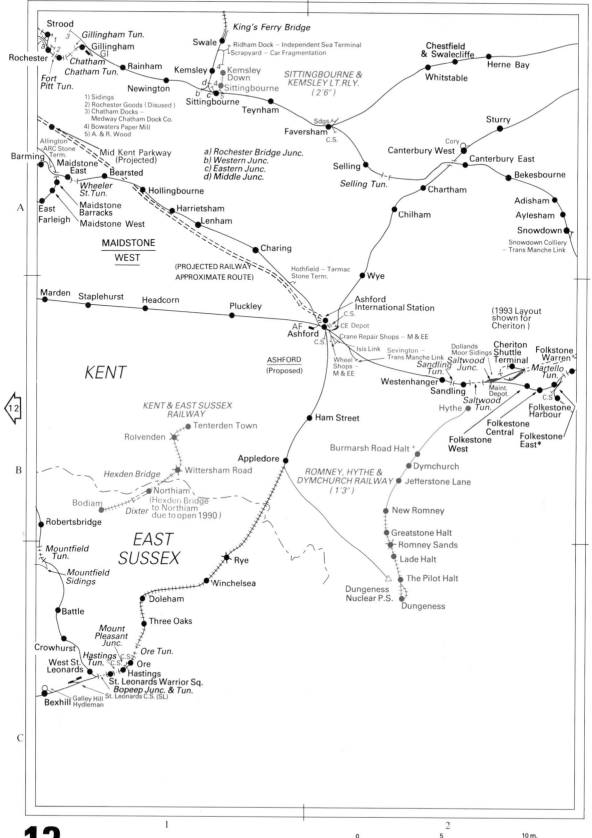
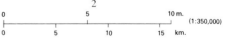

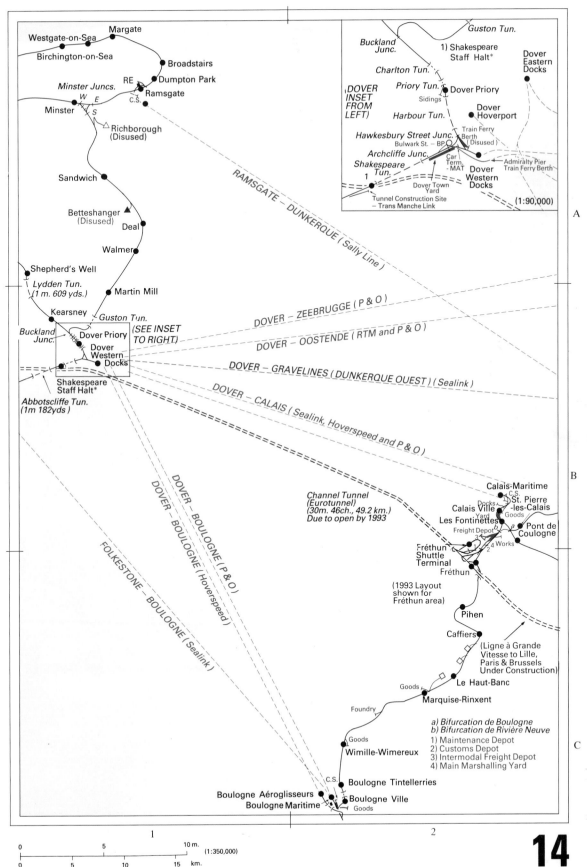

Westgate-on-Sea   Margate

Birchington-on-Sea

Broadstairs

RE   Dumpton Park
Minster Juncs.   Ramsgate
W   E   C.S.
Minster   S

△ Richborough
(Disused)

Sandwich

Betteshanger ▲
(Disused)   Deal

Walmer

Shepherd's Well

Lydden Tun.
(1 m. 609 yds.)   Martin Mill

Kearsney   *Guston Tun.*
(SEE INSET TO RIGHT)
Buckland   Dover Priory
Junc.   Dover Western Docks
Shakespeare Staff Halt*

Abbotscliffe Tun.
(1m 182yds)

RAMSGATE – DUNKERQUE (Sally Line)

DOVER – ZEEBRUGGE (P & O)

DOVER – OOSTENDE (RTM and P & O)

DOVER – GRAVELINES (DUNKERQUE OUEST) (Sealink)

DOVER – CALAIS (Sealink, Hoverspeed and P & O)

DOVER – BOULOGNE (P & O)

DOVER – BOULOGNE (Hoverspeed)

FOLKESTONE – BOULOGNE (Sealink)

Channel Tunnel
(Eurotunnel)
(30m. 46ch., 49.2 km.)
Due to open by 1993

Calais-Maritime
C.S.
St. Pierre
Docks   -les-Calais
Calais Ville   Yard
Les Fontinettes   Goods   a   Pont de
Freight Depot   Coulogne
3   4 Works
Fréthun   1   2
Shuttle
Terminal
Fréthun

(1993 Layout
shown for
Fréthun area)

Pihen

Caffiers ◆

◇   (Ligne à Grande
Vitesse to Lille,
◇   Paris & Brussels
Under Construction)

Goods   Le Haut-Banc

Marquise-Rinxent

Foundry

a) Bifurcation de Boulogne
Goods   b) Bifurcation de Rivière Neuve
Wimille-Wimereux   1) Maintenance Depot
2) Customs Depot
3) Intermodal Freight Depot
4) Main Marshalling Yard

C.S.   Boulogne Tintellieries
Boulogne Aéroglisseurs
Boulogne Ville
Boulogne Maritime   Goods

Inset (top right):

Buckland   *Guston Tun.*
Junc.   1) Shakespeare
Staff Halt*   Dover Eastern Docks
Charlton Tun.
Priory Tun.   Dover Priory
DOVER INSET FROM LEFT)   Sidings
Dover Hoverport
Harbour Tun.

Train Ferry
Hawkesbury Street Junc.   Berth
Bulwark St. – BP ◯   (Disused)
Archcliffe Junc.   Car
Term.   Dover
Shakespeare   – MAT   Western
Tun.   Docks
1   Admiralty Pier
Dover Town   Train Ferry Berth
Yard
Tunnel Construction Site
– Trans Manche Link   (1:90,000)

A

B

C

1   2

0   5   10 m.
0   5   10   15   (1:350,000)
km.

14

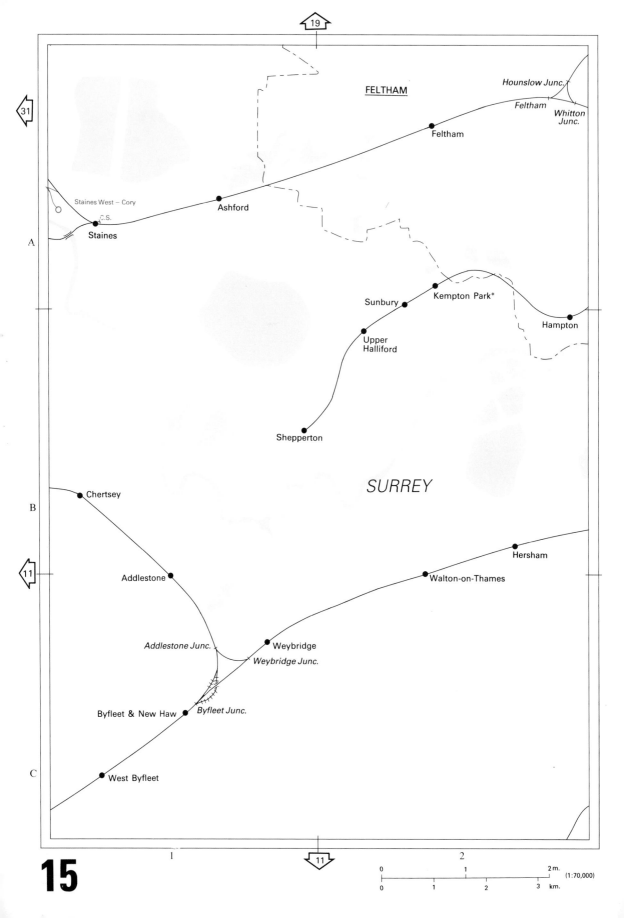

31

FELTHAM

Hounslow Junc.

Feltham

Whitton Junc.

Feltham

Staines West – Cory

C.S.

Ashford

A Staines

Sunbury

Kempton Park*

Upper
Halliford

Hampton

Shepperton

SURREY

Chertsey

B

11

Hersham

Addlestone

Walton-on-Thames

Addlestone Junc.

Weybridge

Weybridge Junc.

Byfleet & New Haw *Byfleet Junc.*

C West Byfleet

2

0   1   2 m.   (1:70,000)

0   1   2   3 km.

15

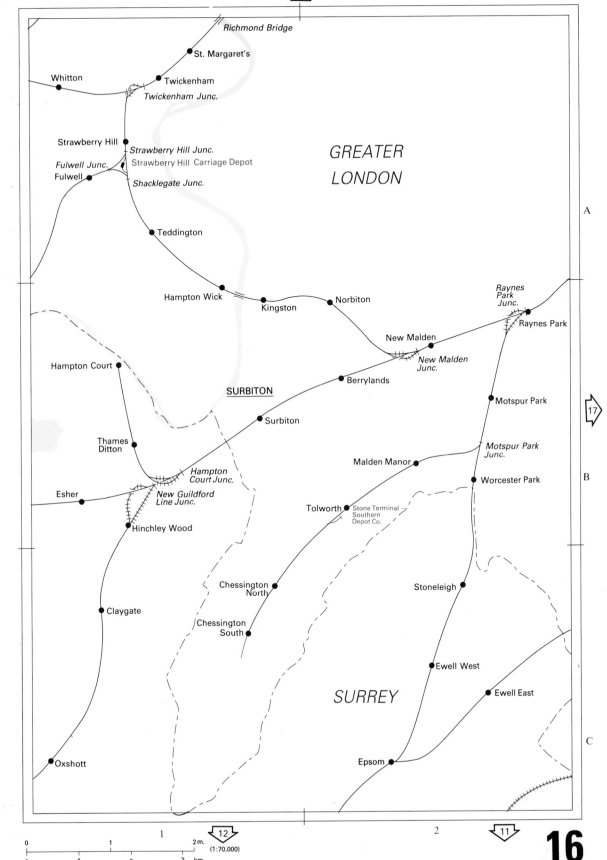

Richmond Bridge

St. Margaret's

Whitton

Twickenham

Twickenham Junc.

Strawberry Hill

Strawberry Hill Junc.

Fulwell Junc.

Strawberry Hill Carriage Depot

Fulwell

Shacklegate Junc.

Teddington

GREATER LONDON

A

Hampton Wick

Kingston

Norbiton

Raynes Park Junc.

Raynes Park

New Malden

New Malden Junc.

Hampton Court

SURBITON

Berrylands

Motspur Park

17

Thames Ditton

Surbiton

Malden Manor

Motspur Park Junc.

Worcester Park

B

Esher

Hampton Court Junc.

New Guildford Line Junc.

Tolworth

Stone Terminal — Southern Depot Co.

Hinchley Wood

Chessington North

Stoneleigh

Claygate

Chessington South

SURREY

Ewell West

Ewell East

C

Oxshott

Epsom

0   1   2 m.

0   1   2   3 km.

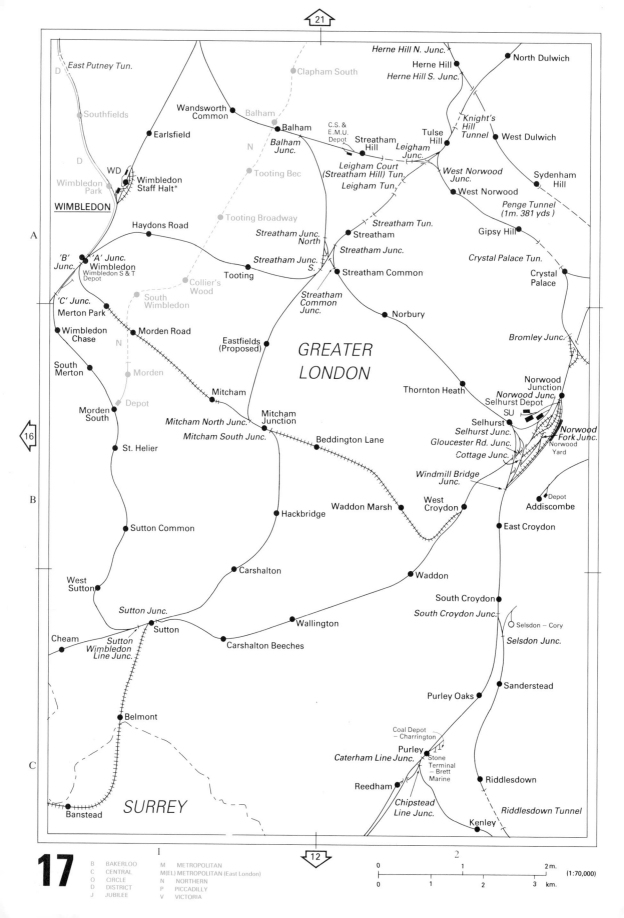

East Putney Tun.

D

Southfields

D

Wimbledon Park

WD

Earlsfield

Wandsworth Common

Balham

Clapham South

Balham

N

Balham Junc.

Tooting Bec

Wimbledon Staff Halt*

WIMBLEDON

Haydons Road

Tooting Broadway

'A' Junc. Wimbledon
Wimbledon S & T Depot

'B' Junc.

Tooting

Collier's Wood

South Wimbledon

'C' Junc. Merton Park

N

Morden

Depot

Wimbledon Chase

Morden Road

Eastfields (Proposed)

South Merton

Morden South

St. Helier

Mitcham

Mitcham Junction

Mitcham North Junc.

Mitcham South Junc.

Beddington Lane

Sutton Common

Hackbridge

Waddon Marsh

Carshalton

West Sutton

Sutton Junc.

Wallington

Cheam

Sutton

Sutton Wimbledon Line Junc.

Carshalton Beeches

Belmont

SURREY

Banstead

C.S. & E.M.U. Depot

Streatham Hill

Leigham Junc.

Leigham Court (Streatham Hill) Tun.

Leigham Tun.

Streatham Junc. North

Streatham

Streatham Tun.

Streatham Junc.

Streatham Junc. S.

Streatham Common

Streatham Common Junc.

Norbury

GREATER LONDON

Thornton Heath

Mitcham Junction

West Croydon

Waddon

South Croydon

South Croydon Junc.

Purley Oaks

Coal Depot – Charrington

Purley

Caterham Line Junc.

Stone Terminal – Brett Marine

Reedham

Chipstead Line Junc.

Kenley

Herne Hill N. Junc.

Herne Hill

Herne Hill S. Junc.

North Dulwich

Tulse Hill

Knight's Hill Tunnel

West Dulwich

West Norwood Junc.

West Norwood

Sydenham Hill

Penge Tunnel (1m. 381 yds)

Gipsy Hill

Crystal Palace Tun.

Crystal Palace

Bromley Junc.

Norwood Junction

Norwood Junc.
Selhurst Depot

SU

Selhurst

Selhurst Junc.

Gloucester Rd. Junc.

Cottage Junc.

Norwood Fork Junc.

Norwood Yard

Windmill Bridge Junc.

Depot

Addiscombe

East Croydon

Selsdon – Cory

Selsdon Junc.

Sanderstead

Riddlesdown

Riddlesdown Tunnel

17

B	BAKERLOO		M	METROPOLITAN
C	CENTRAL		M(EL)	METROPOLITAN (East London)
O	CIRCLE		N	NORTHERN
D	DISTRICT		P	PICCADILLY
J	JUBILEE		V	VICTORIA

0   1   2 m.

0   1   2   3 km.

(1:70,000)

16

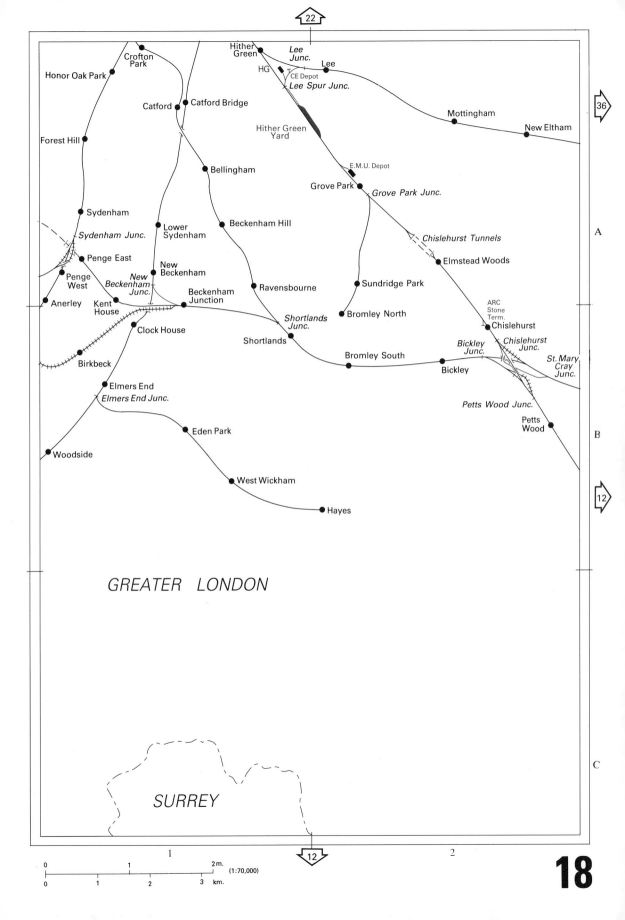

22

Hither Green

Lee Junc.

Lee

HG

CE Depot

Lee Spur Junc.

Crofton Park

Honor Oak Park

Catford

Catford Bridge

Mottingham

New Eltham

36

Hither Green Yard

Forest Hill

Bellingham

E.M.U. Depot

Grove Park

Grove Park Junc.

Sydenham

Sydenham Junc.

Lower Sydenham

Beckenham Hill

Chislehurst Tunnels

A

Penge East

New Beckenham

Elmstead Woods

New Beckenham Junc.

Penge West

Beckenham Junction

Ravensbourne

Sundridge Park

ARC Stone Term.

Chislehurst

Anerley

Kent House

Shortlands Junc.

Bromley North

Chislehurst Junc.

Clock House

Shortlands

Bickley Junc.

St. Mary Cray Junc.

Birkbeck

Bromley South

Bickley

Elmers End

Elmers End Junc.

Petts Wood Junc.

Petts Wood

B

Woodside

Eden Park

12

West Wickham

Hayes

GREATER LONDON

C

SURREY

0   1   2 m.   (1:70,000)

0   1   2   3 km.

18

12

1   2

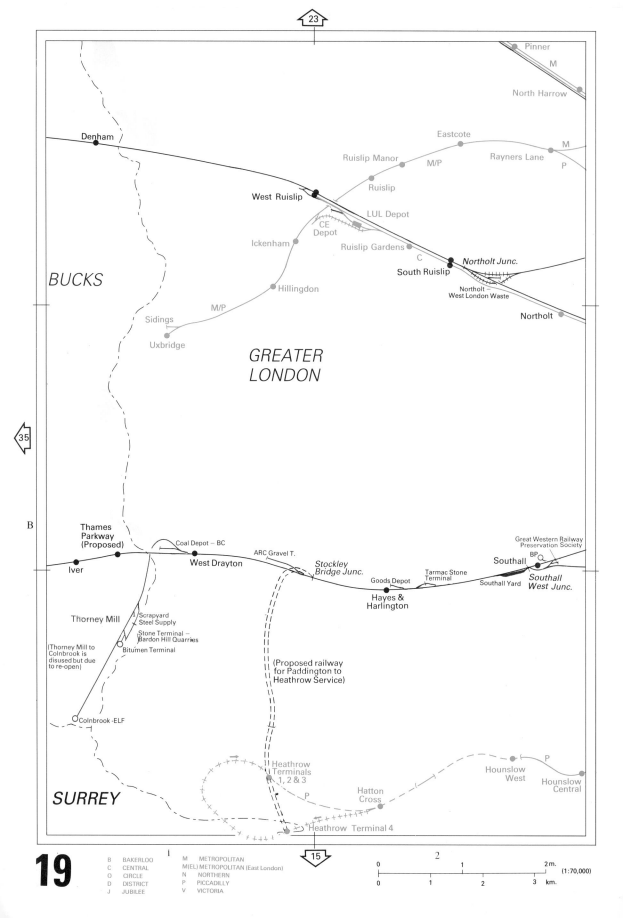

Pinner
M
North Harrow

Denham

Eastcote
Ruislip Manor
M/P
Rayners Lane
M
Ruislip
P

West Ruislip
LUL Depot
CE Depot
Ickenham
Ruislip Gardens
C
Northolt Junc.
South Ruislip
Northolt —
West London Waste
Northolt

BUCKS

Hillingdon
M/P

Sidings
Uxbridge

GREATER LONDON

B

Thames Parkway (Proposed)
Coal Depot – BC
Great Western Railway Preservation Society
ARC Gravel T.
Stockley Bridge Junc.
Southall
BP
Iver
West Drayton
Goods Depot
Tarmac Stone Terminal
Southall Yard
Southall West Junc.
Hayes & Harlington

Thorney Mill
Scrapyard Steel Supply
Stone Terminal – Bardon Hill Quarries
(Proposed railway for Paddington to Heathrow Service)
(Thorney Mill to Colnbrook is disused but due to re-open)
Bitumen Terminal

Colnbrook -ELF

Hounslow West
P
Hounslow Central

Heathrow Terminals 1, 2 & 3
P
Hatton Cross

SURREY

Heathrow Terminal 4

19

B	BAKERLOO	M	METROPOLITAN
C	CENTRAL	M(EL)	METROPOLITAN (East London)
O	CIRCLE	N	NORTHERN
D	DISTRICT	P	PICCADILLY
J	JUBILEE	V	VICTORIA

2

0   1   2 m.
0   1   2   3 km.
(1:70,000)

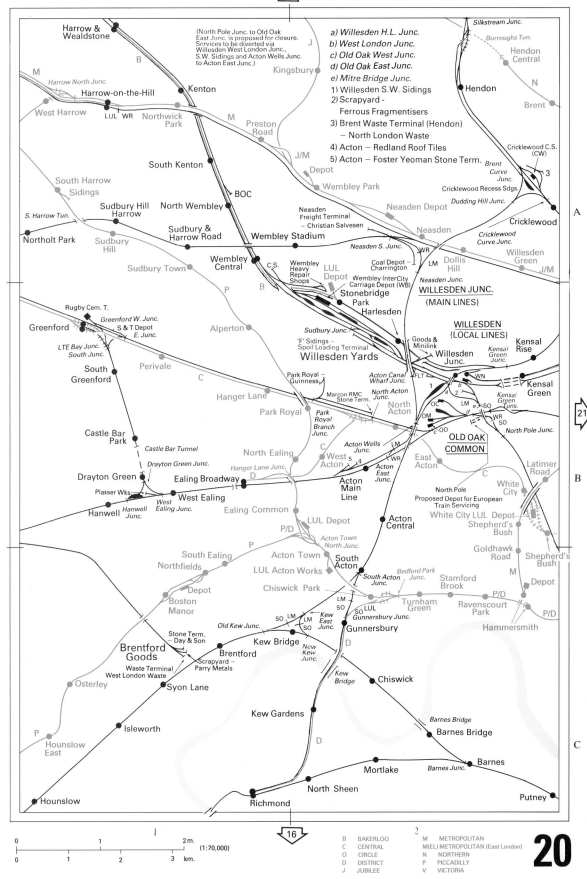

Harrow &
Wealdstone

(North Pole Junc. to Old Oak
Junc. is proposed for closure.
Services to be diverted via
Willesden West London Junc.,
S.W. Sidings and Acton Wells Junc.
to Acton East Junc.)

a) Willesden H.L. Junc.
b) West London Junc.
c) Old Oak West Junc.
d) Old Oak East Junc.
e) Mitre Bridge Junc.
1) Willesden S.W. Sidings
2) Scrapyard -
   Ferrous Fragmentisers
3) Brent Waste Terminal (Hendon)
   − North London Waste
4) Acton − Redland Roof Tiles
5) Acton − Foster Yeoman Stone Term.

Silkstream Junc.
Burroughs Tun.
Hendon
Central
Hendon
Brent
N

B
Kingsbury
J
M
Harrow North Junc.
Kenton
Harrow-on-the-Hill
West Harrow
LUL WR
Northwick
Park
Preston
Road
M
Cricklewood C.S.
(CW)
Brent
Curve
Junc.
3
Cricklewood Recess Sdgs.
Dudding Hill Junc.
A
Cricklewood
South Kenton
Depot
J/M
Wembley Park
Neasden Depot
Neasden
Crickewood
Curve Junc.
Willesden
Green
J/M
South Harrow
Sidings
BOC
North Wembley
Neasden
Freight Terminal
− Christian Salvesen
Neasden S. Junc.
WR
LM
Dollis
Hill
Sudbury Hill
Harrow
Sudbury &
Harrow Road
Wembley Stadium
Neasden Junc.
WILLESDEN JUNC.
(MAIN LINES)
S. Harrow Tun.
Northolt Park
Sudbury
Hill
Wembley
Central
C.S.
Wembley
Heavy
Repair
Shops
LUL
Depot
Coal Depot −
Charrington
Wembley InterCity
Carriage Depot (WB)
WILLESDEN
(LOCAL LINES)
Sudbury Town
P
B
Stonebridge
Park
Harlesden
Kensal
Rise
Rugby Cem. T.
Greenford W. Junc.
S & T Depot
E. Junc.
'F' Sidings −
Spoil Loading Terminal
Goods &
Minilink
Willesden
Junc.
Kensal
Green
Junc.
Kensal
Green
Greenford
LTE Bay Junc.
South Junc.
Alperton
Sudbury Junc.
Willesden Yards
Acton Canal
Wharf Junc.
FLT
WN
South
Greenford
Perivale
C
Park Royal −
Guinness
North Acton
Junc.
1
a b
2
Kensal
Green
Tuns.
Hanger Lane
Park Royal
Marcon RMC
Stone Term.
North
Acton
OC
LM
e SO
Castle Bar
Park
Castle Bar Tunnel
Park
Royal
Branch
Junc.
OM
d
OO
WR
SO
North Pole Junc.
Drayton Green Junc.
North Ealing
West
Acton
5
Acton
East
Junc.
LM
WR
East
Acton
OLD OAK
COMMON
Latimer
Road
Drayton Green
Ealing Broadway
Hanger Lane Junc.
Acton Wells
Junc.
4
North Pole
Proposed Depot for European
Train Servicing
C
White
City
B
Plasser Wks.
West
Ealing Junc.
West Ealing
D
Acton
Main
Line
White City LUL Depot
Shepherd's
Bush
Hanwell
Hanwell
Junc.
Ealing Common
Acton
Central
Goldhawk
Road
Shepherd's
Bush
M
Depot
LUL Depot
P/D
South Ealing
Northfields
Acton Town
North Junc.
South
Acton
Bedford Park
Junc.
Stamford
Brook
Ravenscourt
Park
P/D
P
Depot
Boston
Manor
Chiswick Park
LUL Acton Works
South Acton
Junc.
Turnham
Green
SO LUL
P/D
Hammersmith
Old Kew Junc.
Kew
East
Junc.
LM
SO
Gunnersbury Junc.
Stone Term. −
Day & Son
Kew Bridge
SO LM
LM
SO
Gunnersbury
Brentford
Goods
Brentford
New
Kew
Junc.
Waste Terminal
West London Waste
Scrapyard −
Parry Metals
Kew
Bridge
Chiswick
D
Osterley
Syon Lane
Kew Gardens
Barnes Bridge
Barnes Bridge
C
P
Isleworth
D
Barnes Junc.
Barnes
Hounslow
East
Mortlake
North Sheen
Hounslow
Richmond
Putney

0   1   2 m.
| | | |
0   1   2   3 km.   (1:70,000)

1   2

B   BAKERLOO   M   METROPOLITAN
C   CENTRAL   M(EL) METROPOLITAN (East London)
O   CIRCLE   N   NORTHERN
D   DISTRICT   P   PICCADILLY
J   JUBILEE   V   VICTORIA

20

21

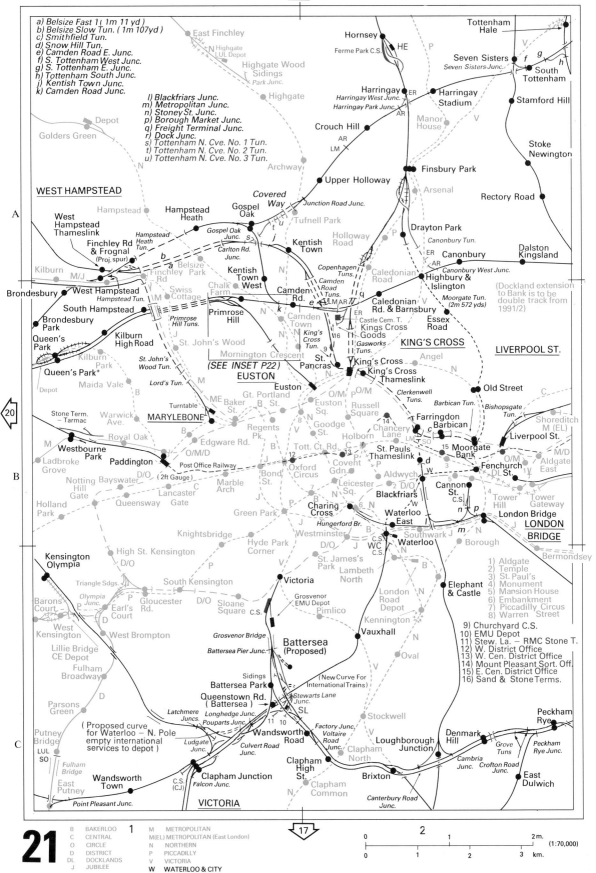

Blackhorse Rd. Wood St. Barkingside

St. James Street Walthamstow Central Walthamstow Queens Road

Copper Mill Junc. Hall Farm Junc. (Proposed Curve)

Snaresbrook Wanstead Redbridge Gants Hill Newbury Park

Lea Bridge Junc.

Clapton Junc.

GREATER LONDON

Leyton Midland Road

Leytonstone

Clapton

Clapton Tun.

Queens Road Tun.

Leytonstone High Rd.

IL

Ilford

C.S.

Hackney Downs N. Junc.

CE Sidings

Temple Mills Yard

Leyton Leyton CE Yard

Wanstead Park Manor Park

Forest Gate Junc.

Woodgrange Park

A

Hackney Downs Homerton

Stratford FLT Temple Mills E. Junc.

High Meads Junc.

LIFT & Isis Link SR

Hackney Central Hackney Wick SF

Lea Junc. Maryland

Forest Gate

Woodgrange Park Junc.

Barking Stn. Junc.

Barking Trust Estates

EM

Barking

C.S.

Reading Lane Junc.

C.S.

London Fields

h g d

a

Stratford

C.S.

East Ham

M/D

Barking Tilbury Line Junc. West

Barking Tilbury Line Junc. East

Rugby Cem. Term. TF Thornton Fields C.S.

c

b

Cambridge Heath

Coal Depot

Bow Goods

ECC Stone Terminal

Upton Park

Pudding Mill Lane (Proposed Station)

a) Carpenters Rd. N. Junc.

b) Carpenters Rd. S. Junc.

Bethnal Green

Bow Junc.

Carless

Plaistow

c) Stratford Southern Junc.

d) Stratford Central Junc.

Mile End – Tarmac Stone Term.

DL

West Ham

e) Charlton Junc.

f) South Bermondsey Junc.

Bethnal Green E. Junc.

Bow Rd.

M/D Mile End

Bow Church

Bow Junc.

Steetley Chem Wks.

(Projected BR West Ham)

g) Channelsea S. Junc.

h) Channelsea N. Junc.

j) Navarino Road Junc.

k) Gas Factory Junc.

Bethnal Green

Stepney Green

Devons Road

k

Bromley -by-Bow

West Ham

J

(Docklands Light Railway extension under construction – to open 1992)

Whitechapel

Eastern District Office

DL

Canning Town

DL

Custom House Victoria Dock (Proposed)

Prince Regent

Beckton Depot

Limehouse

Poplar Maintenance Depot

All Saints

DL

Thames Wharf (Projected)

Royal Albert

Beckton Park

Beckton

DL

Shadwell

M (EL)

Westferry West India Quay

Brunswick

DL

Custom House

Connaught (Projected)

Cyprus (Projected)

Gallions Reach

B

Wapping

Canary Wharf

Poplar

Blackwall

Royal Victoria (Proposed)

Silvertown Tun.

Rotherhithe J

Heron Quays

DL

Silvertown

North Woolwich

Scrapyard Ward Ferrous Metals

South Quay

(Proposed extension)

Woolwich Free Ferry

J

Canada Water (Proposed)

Crossharbour

Angerstein Wharf

Marcon RMC Stone Loading Terminal

Dock St. Tun.

Coleman St. Tun.

George IV Tun.

Calderwood St. Tun. Cross St. Tun.

Goods Sdgs.

Southwark Park Junc.

Surrey Quays

M (EL)

Mudchute

DL

Mount St. Tun.

Charlton Tun.

Woolwich Dockyard

Woolwich Arsenal

Plumstead

f

Surrey Canal Junc.

Island Gardens

Westcombe Park

Charlton

e

Primrose Hill

Camden Road Junc.

South Bermondsey

North Kent East Junc.

(Pedestrian Tunnel)

Maze Hill

CE Works

Angerstein Junc.

Camden Juncs.

Camden Carriage Sidings

Camden Road

LUL Depot

Deptford

Greenwich College Tun.

Primrose Hill Tuns.

Up Empty Carriage Line Tun.

Camden Town

New Cross Gate C.S.

New Cross

Greenwich

Blackheath Tunnel

(INSET FROM MAP 21) (1:35,000)

Park St. Tuns.

Morn. Cres.

Queens Road (Peckham)

New Cross Gate

Tanners Hill Junc.

St. John's

Blackheath Junc.

Kidbrooke Tun.

(Primrose Hill Tuns. to Primrose Hill & Camden Rd. proposed for closure to passengers)

Up Empty Carriage Shed

EN

Nunhead

Lewisham Vale Junc.

Blackheath

Down Empty Carriage Shed

(TO EUSTON)

C

Nunhead Junc.

Brockley

Parks Bridge Junc.

Lewisham

Kidbrooke

Falconwood

Ladywell Junc.

Courthill Loop North

Courthill Loop Junc. South

Eltham

Ladywell

36

B	BAKERLOO	M	METROPOLITAN
C	CENTRAL	M(EL)	METROPOLITAN (East London)
O	CIRCLE	N	NORTHERN
D	DISTRICT	P	PICCADILLY
DL	DOCKLANDS	V	VICTORIA
J	JUBILEE		

0 1 2 m. (1:70,000)

0 1 2 3 km.

22

(Stratford Central Junction to Channelsea South Junction and Navarino Road Junction to Reading Lane Junction are proposed for closure to passengers)

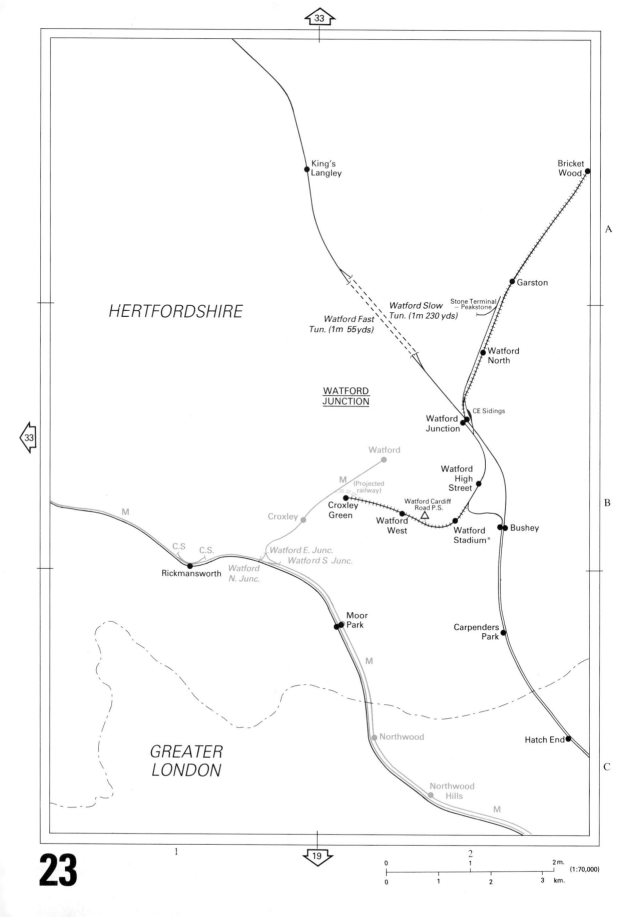

Bricket
Wood

King's
Langley

A

HERTFORDSHIRE

Garston

Stone Terminal
— Peakstone

Watford Slow
Tun. (1m 230 yds)

Watford Fast
Tun. (1m 55 yds)

Watford
North

WATFORD
JUNCTION

CE Sidings

Watford
Junction

Watford

M

(Projected
railway)

Watford
High
Street

B

Croxley

Croxley
Green

Watford Cardiff
Road P.S.

Watford
West

Watford
Stadium*

Bushey

M

C.S

C.S.

Watford E. Junc.
Watford S. Junc.

Rickmansworth

Watford
N. Junc.

Moor
Park

Carpenders
Park

M

Northwood

Hatch End

C

GREATER
LONDON

Northwood
Hills

M

23

0		1		2 m.

(1:70,000)

| 0 | 1 | 2 | 3 | km. |

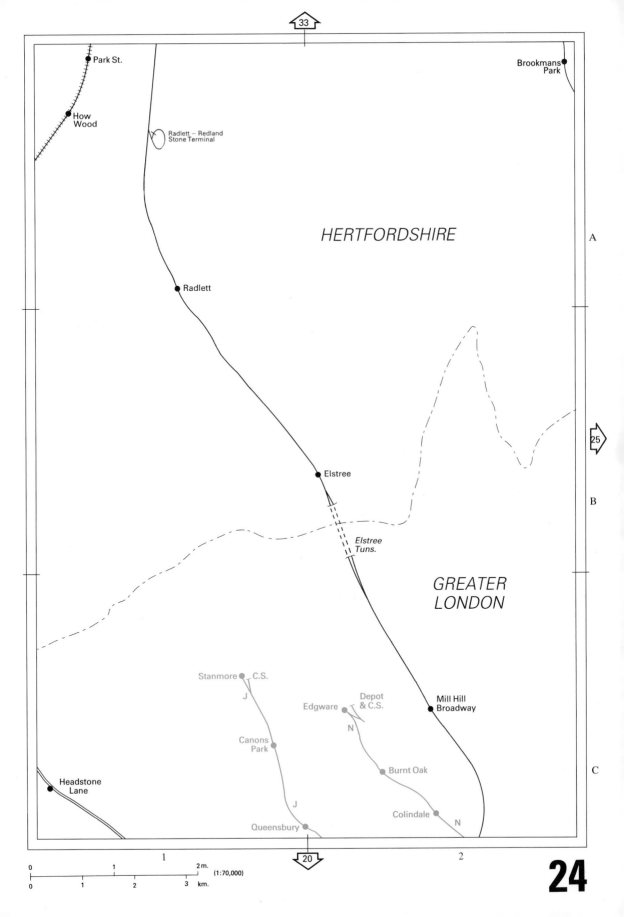

Park St.

Brookmans Park

How
Wood

Radlett – Redland
Stone Terminal

HERTFORDSHIRE

Radlett

25

Elstree

B

Elstree
Tuns.

GREATER
LONDON

Stanmore C.S.

J

Depot
& C.S.

Edgware

N

Mill Hill
Broadway

Canons
Park

Burnt Oak

Headstone
Lane

C

J

Colindale N

Queensbury

1

2

0   1   2 m.   (1:70,000)
0   1   2   3   km.

24

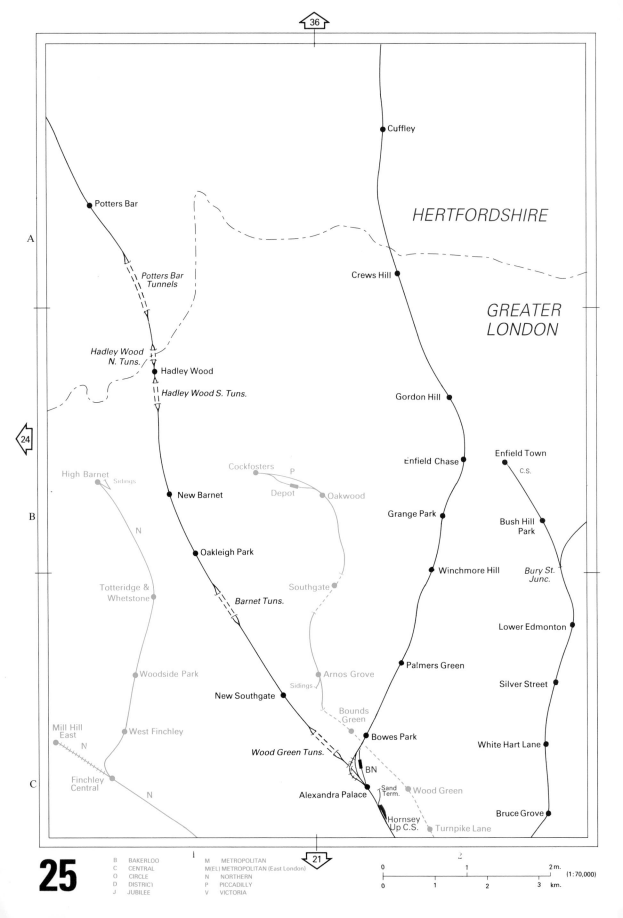

Cuffley

HERTFORDSHIRE

Potters Bar

A

*Potters Bar
Tunnels*

Crews Hill

*GREATER
LONDON*

*Hadley Wood
N. Tuns.*

Hadley Wood

Hadley Wood S. Tuns.

Gordon Hill

24

Enfield Town

C.S.

Cockfosters   P

Enfield Chase

High Barnet   Sidings

Depot   Oakwood

New Barnet

B   Grange Park

Bush Hill
Park

N

Oakleigh Park

*Bury St.
Junc.*

Winchmore Hill

Totteridge &
Whetstone

Barnet Tuns.

Southgate

Lower Edmonton

Woodside Park

Palmers Green

Arnos Grove

Silver Street

New Southgate   Sidings

Mill Hill
East

Bounds
Green

West Finchley   N

Wood Green Tuns.   Bowes Park

White Hart Lane

BN

C   Finchley
Central   N

Sand
Term.   Wood Green

Alexandra Palace

Bruce Grove

Hornsey
Up C.S.   Turnpike Lane

25

B	BAKERLOO		M	METROPOLITAN
C	CENTRAL		M(EL)	METROPOLITAN (East London)
O	CIRCLE		N	NORTHERN
D	DISTRICT		P	PICCADILLY
J	JUBILEE		V	VICTORIA

0   1   2 m.

0   1   2   3 km.   (1 : 70,000)

Cheshunt
Cheshunt Junc.

Theobalds
Grove

A

Waltham
Cross

ESSEX

Turkey
Street

Enfield
Lock

36

Brimsdown

Debden

Loughton

C

B

Southbury

Ponders End

Chingford

C.S.

Buckhurst Hill

Chigwell

Roding Valley

Grange Hill

LUL Depot

Angel Road

Highams Park

Woodford

Sidings

Hainault

Northumberland Park

Fairlop

C

Northumberland Park
LUL Depot and Staff Halt*

South Woodford

22

| 1 | | 2m. | | | 2 | | |
0   1   2   (1:70,000)

0   1   2   3   km.

B	BAKERLOO	M	METROPOLITAN
C	CENTRAL	M(EL)	METROPOLITAN (East London)
O	CIRCLE	N	NORTHERN
D	DISTRICT	P	PICCADILLY
J	JUBILEE	V	VICTORIA

26

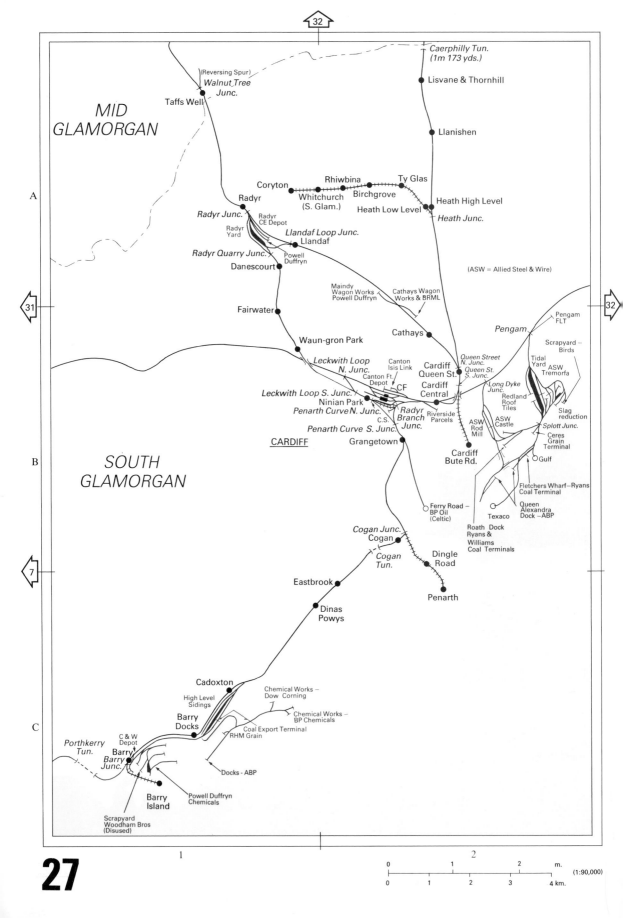

MID
GLAMORGAN

Caerphilly Tun.
(1m 173 yds.)

Lisvane & Thornhill

Walnut Tree
(Reversing Spur)
Junc.

Taffs Well

Llanishen

Coryton
Rhiwbina
Ty Glas

Radyr
Whitchurch
(S. Glam.)
Birchgrove
Heath High Level

Radyr Junc.
Radyr
CE Depot
Heath Low Level
Heath Junc.

Radyr
Yard
Llandaf Loop Junc.

Radyr Quarry Junc.
Powell
Duffryn
Llandaf

Danescourt
(ASW = Allied Steel & Wire)

Maindy
Wagon Works
Powell Duffryn
Cathays Wagon
Works & BRML

Fairwater
Pengam
FLT

Pengam

Waun-gron Park
Scrapyard –
Birds

Leckwith Loop
N. Junc.
Canton
Isis Link
Queen Street
N. Junc.
Cardiff
Queen St.
Queen St.
S. Junc.
Tidal
Yard
ASW
Tremorfa

Canton Ft.
Depot
CF
Cardiff
Central
Long Dyke
Junc.

Leckwith Loop S. Junc.
Redland
Roof
Tiles
Slag
reduction

Ninian Park
Radyr
Branch
Junc.
Riverside
Parcels
ASW
Castle

Penarth Curve N. Junc.
C.S.
Splott Junc.

Penarth Curve S. Junc.
ASW
Rod
Mill
Ceres
Grain
Terminal

SOUTH
GLAMORGAN
CARDIFF
Grangetown
Cardiff
Bute Rd.
Gulf

Fletchers Wharf–Ryans
Coal Terminal

Ferry Road –
BP Oil
(Celtic)
Texaco
Queen
Alexandra
Dock –ABP

Roath Dock
Ryans &
Williams
Coal Terminals

Cogan Junc.
Cogan
Dingle
Road

Cogan Tun.

Eastbrook
Penarth

Dinas
Powys

Cadoxton

Chemical Works –
Dow Corning

High Level
Sidings
Chemical Works –
BP Chemicals

Barry
Docks
Coal Export Terminal
RHM Grain

Porthkerry Tun.
C & W
Depot
Docks - ABP

Barry
Barry
Junc.

Barry
Island
Powell Duffryn
Chemicals

Scrapyard
Woodham Bros
(Disused)

27

0   1   2   m.

0   1   2   3   4 km.   (1:90,000)

1   2

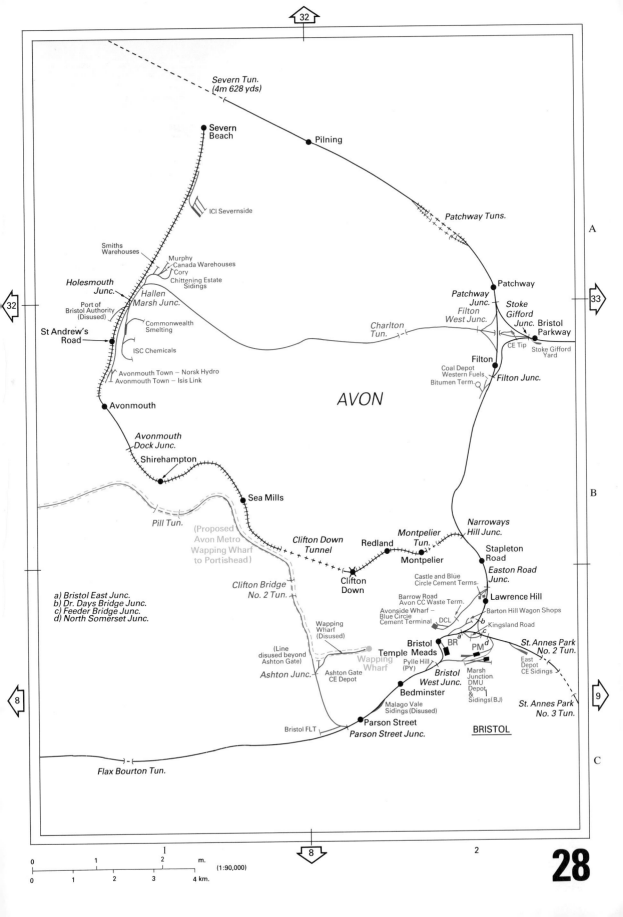

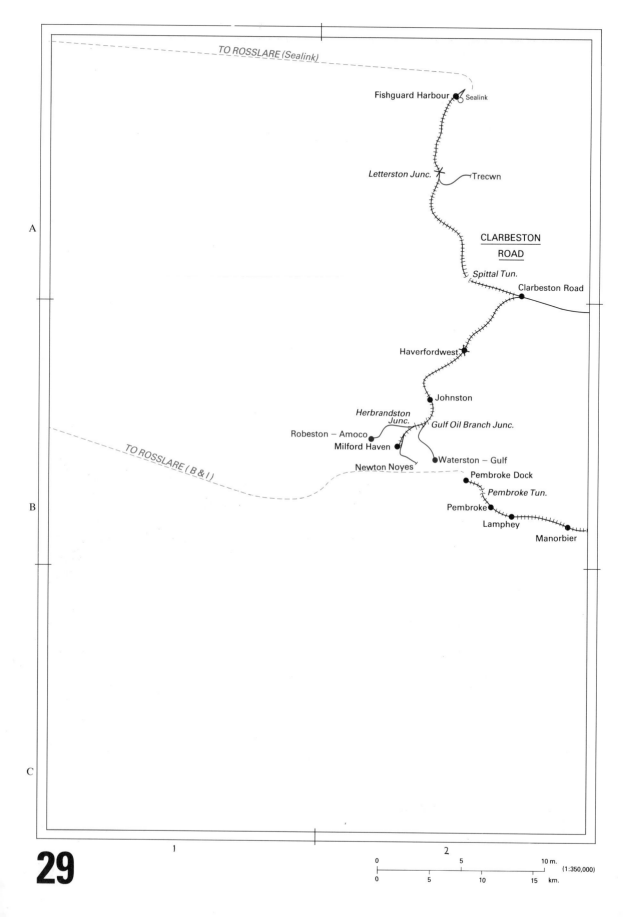

TO ROSSLARE *(Sealink)*

Fishguard Harbour ● ○ Sealink

Letterston Junc. ✕ ⌐ Trecwn

CLARBESTON
ROAD

Spittal Tun.

Clarbeston Road ●

Haverfordwest ◆

Johnston ●

Herbrandston
Junc.

Gulf Oil Branch Junc.

Robeston – Amoco ●

Milford Haven ●

Waterston – Gulf ●

TO ROSSLARE *(B & I)*

Newton Noyes

Pembroke Dock ●

Pembroke Tun.

Pembroke ●

Lamphey ●

Manorbier ●

A

B

C

1

2

0   5   10 m.

0   5   10   15   km.

(1:350,000)

29

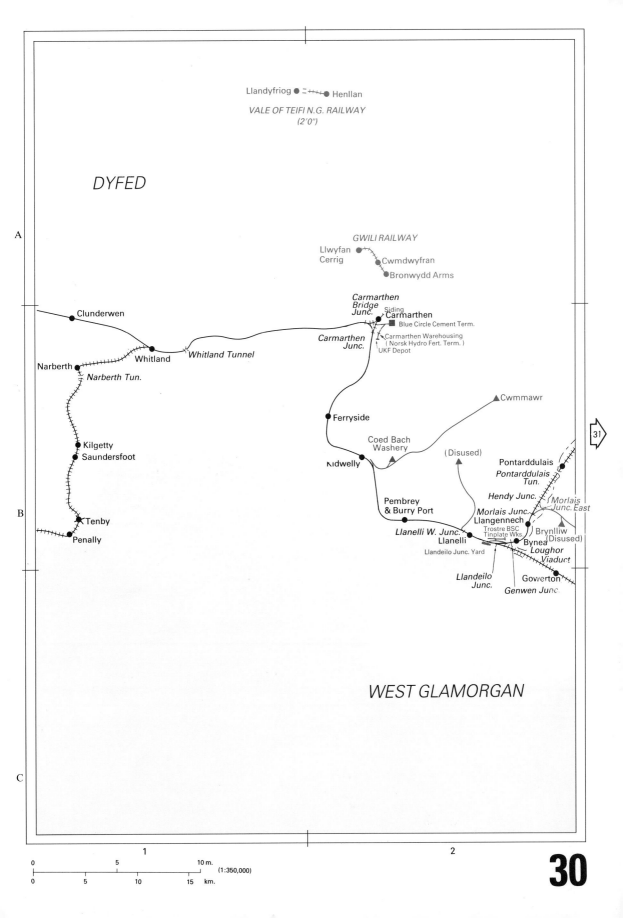

Llandyfriog ● ☰╫╫╫● Henllan

VALE OF TEIFI N.G. RAILWAY
(2'0")

DYFED

A

GWILI RAILWAY
Llwyfan ●
Cerrig   ●Cwmdwyfran
              ●Bronwydd Arms

Carmarthen
Bridge
Junc.   Siding
            ●Carmarthen
            ■ Blue Circle Cement Term.
Carmarthen   Carmarthen Warehousing
Junc.   (Norsk Hydro Fert. Term.)
              UKF Depot

Clunderwen

▲Cwmmawr

Narberth   Whitland Tunnel
Whitland
Narberth Tun.   Ferryside

                    Coed Bach
                    Washery   (Disused)
                                            ▲   Pontarddulais
Kilgetty   *Pontarddulais*
Saunderstoot   Kidwelly   ▲   *Tun.*

                                               Hendy Junc.   *(Morlais*
B   Pembrey   *Junc. East*
                    & Burry Port   *Morlais Junc.*
▲Tenby   Llangennech
Penally   *Llanelli W. Junc.* Trostre BSC   *Brynlliw*
                    Llanelli   Tinplate Wks.   Bynea *(Disused)*
                    Llandeilo Junc. Yard   *Loughor*
                                                      Viaduct
                    Llandeilo   Gowerton
                    Junc.   *Genwen Junc.*

31

WEST GLAMORGAN

C

1   2

0   5   10 m.   (1:350,000)
0   5   10   15   km.

30

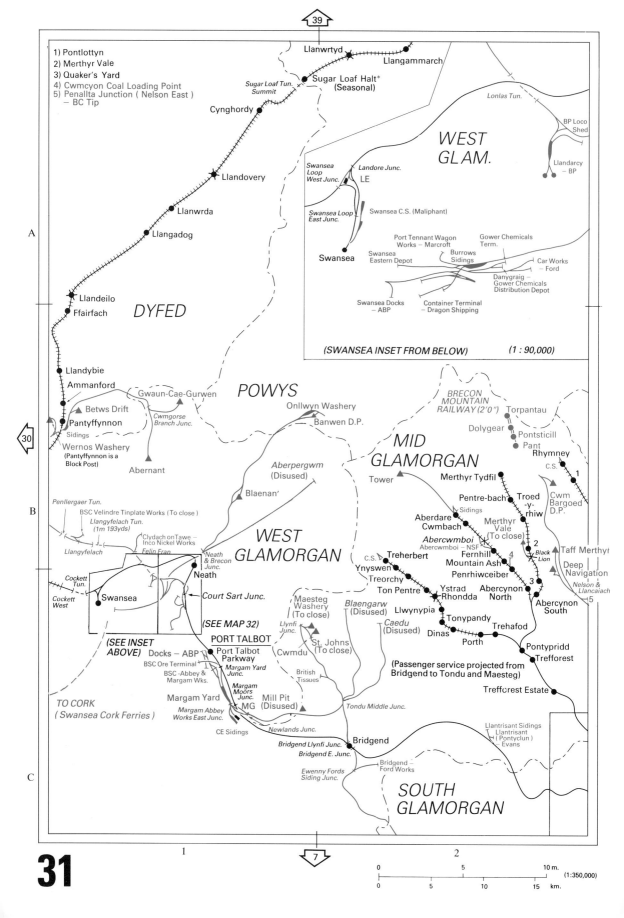

1) Pontlottyn
2) Merthyr Vale
3) Quaker's Yard
4) Cwmcyon Coal Loading Point
5) Penallta Junction (Nelson East)
— BC Tip

Llanwrtyd
Llangammarch

Sugar Loaf Tun.
Summit
Sugar Loaf Halt*
(Seasonal)

WEST
GLAM.

Lonlas Tun.

BP Loco
Shed

Cynghordy

Swansea Loop
West Junc.
Landore Junc.
LE

Llandarcy
— BP

Llandovery

Swansea Loop
East Junc.
Swansea C.S. (Maliphant)

Llanwrda

Port Tennant Wagon
Works — Marcroft
Gower Chemicals
Term.

Llangadog

A

Swansea
Swansea
Eastern Depot
Burrows
Sidings
Car Works
— Ford

DYFED
Danygraig —
Gower Chemicals
Distribution Depot

Llandeilo
Ffairfach

Swansea Docks
— ABP
Container Terminal
— Dragon Shipping

(SWANSEA INSET FROM BELOW)
(1 : 90,000)

POWYS

Llandybie
Ammanford

Gwaun-Cae-Gurwen

Onllwyn Washery
Banwen D.P.

*BRECON
MOUNTAIN
RAILWAY (2'0")*
Torpantau

Betws Drift

Cwmgorse
Branch Junc.

Dolygear
Pontsticill
Pant

Rhymney

30

Pantyffynnon
Sidings

*MID
GLAMORGAN*

C.S.
1

Wernos Washery
(Pantyffynnon is a
Block Post)
Abernant

Aberpergwm
(Disused)

Tower

Merthyr Tydfil

Cwm
Bargoed
D.P.

Pentre-bach

Blaenan'

Sidings

Troed
-y-
rhiw

B

Penllergaer Tun.
BSC Velindre Tinplate Works (To close)

Aberdare
Cwmbach

Merthyr
Vale
(To close)

Taff Merthyr

2

Llangyfelach Tun.
(1m 193yds)

*WEST
GLAMORGAN*

Abercwmboi
Abercwmboi — NSF
Fernhill
4

Black
Lion

Deep
Navigation

Clydach on Tawe —
Inco Nickel Works
Felin Fran

C.S.
Treherbert

Mountain Ash
Penrhiwceiber

3

Llangyfelach

Neath
& Brecon
Junc.
Neath

Ynyswen
Treorchy

Abercynon
North

*Nelson &
Llancaiach*
5

*Cockett
Tun.*

Ton Pentre

Ystrad
Rhondda

Abercynon
South

*Cockett
West*

Swansea

Court Sart Junc.

Llwynypia

Treorchy

Tonypandy

Trehafod

Pontypridd
Trefforest

(SEE MAP 32)

Maesteg
Washery
(To close)
Blaengarw
(Disused)
Dinas
Porth

*(SEE INSET
ABOVE)*
PORT TALBOT
Docks — ABP
Port Talbot
Parkway

Llynfi
Junc.
Caedu
(Disused)

*(Passenger service projected from
Bridgend to Tondu and Maesteg)*

BSC Ore Terminal
BSC -Abbey &
Margam Wks.

St. Johns
(To close)

Cwmdu

British
Tissues

Trefforest Estate

*Margam Yard
Junc.*

Margam Yard

*Margam
Moors
Junc.*
MG

Mill Pit
(Disused)

Tondu Middle Junc.

Llantrisant Sidings
Llantrisant
(Pontyclun)
Evans

*Margam Abbey
Works East Junc.*

CE Sidings

Newlands Junc.

Bridgend Llynfi Junc.
Bridgend E. Junc.
Bridgend

*TO CORK
(Swansea Cork Ferries)*

*Ewenny Fords
Siding Junc.*
*Bridgend
Ford Works*

*SOUTH
GLAMORGAN*

C

7

0		5		10 m.

(1:350,000)

0	5	10	15

km.

1
2

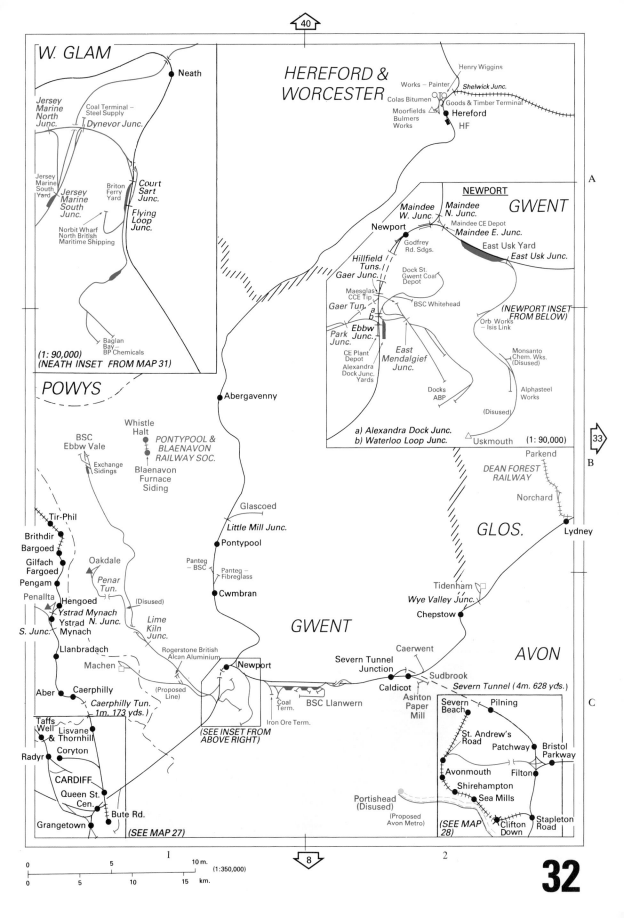

W. GLAM

● Neath

Jersey Marine North Junc.

Coal Terminal – Steel Supply

Dynevor Junc.

Jersey Marine South Yard

Jersey Marine South Junc.

Briton Ferry Yard

Court Sart Junc.

Flying Loop Junc.

Norbit Wharf North British Maritime Shipping

Baglan Bay – BP Chemicals

(1: 90,000)
(NEATH INSET FROM MAP 31)

POWYS

HEREFORD & WORCESTER

Henry Wiggins

Works – Painter

Shelwick Junc.

Colas Bitumen

Goods & Timber Terminal

Moorfields Bulmers Works

△ ● Hereford

HF

NEWPORT

GWENT

Maindee W. Junc.

Maindee N. Junc.

Maindee CE Depot

● Newport

Maindee E. Junc.

Godfrey Rd. Sdgs.

East Usk Yard

East Usk Junc.

Hillfield Tuns. /

Dock St. Gwent Coal Depot

Gaer Junc.

Maesglas CCE Tip

BSC Whitehead

Gaer Tun.

a
b

Park Junc.

Ebbw Junc.

East Mendalgief Junc.

(NEWPORT INSET FROM BELOW)

Orb Works – Isis Link

Monsanto Chem. Wks. (Disused)

CE Plant Depot

Alexandra Dock Junc. Yards

Docks ABP

Alphasteel Works

(Disused)

a) Alexandra Dock Junc.
b) Waterloo Loop Junc.

△ Uskmouth

(1: 90,000)

● Abergavenny

Whistle Halt

PONTYPOOL & BLAENAVON RAILWAY SOC.

BSC Ebbw Vale

Exchange Sidings

Blaenavon Furnace Siding

Glascoed

Little Mill Junc.

● Tir-Phil

● Brithdir

Bargoed

Gilfach Fargoed

Pengam

● Pontypool

Oakdale

Penar Tun.

Panteg – BSC

Panteg – Fibreglass

Penallta

● Cwmbran

Ystrad Mynach N. Junc.

Ystrad Mynach

(Disused)

Lime Kiln Junc.

S. Junc.

● Hengoed

● Llanbradach

Rogerstone British Alcan Aluminium

GWENT

Parkend

DEAN FOREST RAILWAY

Norchard

GLOS.

● Lydney

● Tidenham □

Wye Valley Junc.

● Chepstow

AVON

Caerwent

Severn Tunnel Junction

Machen □

(Proposed Line)

● Newport

Aber ●

● Caerphilly

Caerphilly Tun. 1m. 173 yds.

(SEE INSET FROM ABOVE RIGHT)

Coal Term.

BSC Llanwern

Iron Ore Term.

Caldicot ●

Sudbrook

Ashton Paper Mill

Caerwent

Severn Tunnel (4m. 628 yds.)

Taffs Well

Lisvane & Thornhill

Coryton

Radyr ●

CARDIFF

Queen St. Cen.

Grangetown ●

● Bute Rd.

(SEE MAP 27)

Severn Beach

● Pilning

St. Andrew's Road

● Patchway

Bristol Parkway

● Avonmouth

Filton

Shirehampton

● Sea Mills

Portishead (Disused)

(Proposed Avon Metro)

★ Clifton Down

Stapleton Road

(SEE MAP 28)

0 ___ 5 ___ 10 m.

(1:350,000)

0 ___ 5 ___ 10 ___ 15 km.

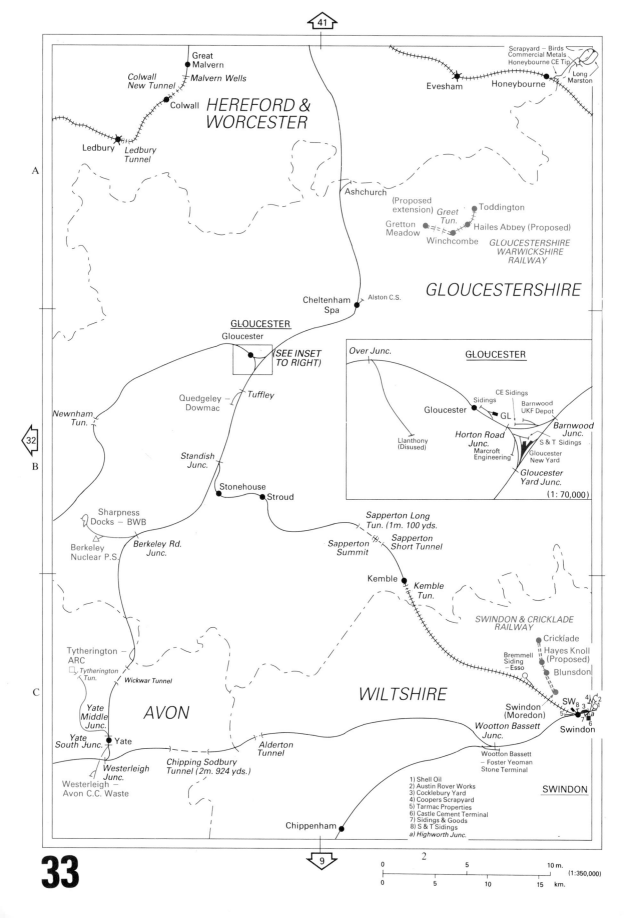

Great
Malvern
Malvern Wells
Colwall
New Tunnel
Colwall

HEREFORD &
WORCESTER

Ledbury
Ledbury
Tunnel

Scrapyard – Birds
Commercial Metals
Honeybourne CE Tip

Evesham
Honeybourne
Long
Marston

A

Ashchurch

(Proposed
extension)   *Greet*   Toddington
Tun.
Gretton   Hailes Abbey (Proposed)
Meadow
Winchcombe
GLOUCESTERSHIRE
WARWICKSHIRE
RAILWAY

GLOUCESTERSHIRE

Cheltenham   Alston C.S.
Spa

GLOUCESTER
Gloucester
(SEE INSET
TO RIGHT)

Quedgeley –   *Tuffley*
Dowmac

Newnham
Tun.

GLOUCESTER

Over Junc.

CE Sidings
Sidings   Barnwood
Gloucester   GL   UKF Depot
Barnwood
Junc.
S & T Sidings
Llanthony   *Horton Road*
(Disused)   *Junc.*   Gloucester
Marcroft   New Yard
Engineering
Gloucester
Yard Junc.

(1 : 70,000)

Standish
Junc.

Stonehouse
Stroud

Sharpness
Docks – BWB
Sapperton Long
Tun. (1m. 100 yds.
Sapperton   *Sapperton*
Summit   *Short Tunnel*

Berkeley
Nuclear P.S.   *Berkeley Rd.*
Junc.
Kemble   *Kemble*
Tun.

SWINDON & CRICKLADE
RAILWAY

Cricklade

Tytherington –   Bremmell   Hayes Knoll
ARC   Siding   (Proposed)
Tytherington   – Esso
Tun.   *Wickwar Tunnel*   Blunsdon

C

Yate   # WILTSHIRE
Middle
Junc.   Swindon   SW 4
Yate   Yate   (Moredon)   8 3 2
South Junc.   *Wootton Bassett*   5 7 a
Alderton   *Junc.*   Swindon
Tunnel   6
Westerleigh
Junc.   *Chipping Sodbury Tunnel (2m. 924 yds.)*   Wootton Bassett
Westerleigh –   – Foster Yeoman
Avon C.C. Waste   Stone Terminal
SWINDON

AVON

1) Shell Oil
2) Austin Rover Works
3) Cocklebury Yard
4) Coopers Scrapyard
5) Tarmac Properties
6) Castle Cement Terminal
7) Sidings & Goods
8) S & T Sidings
a) Highworth Junc.

Chippenham

33

2
0   5   10 m.
(1:350,000)
0   5   10   15 km.

WARWICKSHIRE

NORTHAMPTONSHIRE

BUCKS

Campden Tun.

Moreton-in-Marsh

Foster-Yeoman and Redland Stone Terminals

Banbury Yard

Banbury

Sidings

BP

Kings Sutton

Aynho Junc.

Aynho Park Junc.

Ardley Tunnel

OXFORDSHIRE

A

Heyford

Kingham

Shipton

Charlbury

Finstock

Ascott-under-Wychwood

Combe

Tackley

Bletchington Blue Circle Cem. Works

Bicester North

Bicester Town

BICESTER MIL. RLY.

Arncott

Brill Tun.

Handborough

Islip – Esso (Disused)

Islip

Banbury Road ARC Stone Term.

Wolvercot Junc.

Wolvercote Tun.

Oxford North Junc.

Appleford

35

C.S.

OX

Scrapyard – Hebborns

Becket St. Coal Depot

Oxford

Esso

Austin Rover

Morris Cowley

OXFORD

B

ARC Stone Term. & Waste Term.

Hinksey Yard

Kennington Junc.

MAT Car Terminal

Freight Depot

Cowley Freight Terminals Ltd

Didcot Distribution Centre (Milton) – Lansdown International Facilities

Didcot

Didcot West Curve Junc.

CE Tip

Didcot North Junc.

Great Western Society

Littlemore – BP Oil (Hartwells)

Radley

Foxhall Junc.

Steventon Bulk Haulage

Didcot West Junc.

Didcot Parkway

Didcot East Junc.

Didcot Yard

(1 : 70,000)

Culham

Appleford

Didcot Parkway

Wallingford

CHOLSEY & WALLINGFORD RAILWAY

Cholsey

Goring & Streatley

C

BERKSHIRE

Pangbourne

Tilehurst

1

2

0   5   10 m.

(1 : 350,000)

0   5   10   15 km.

34

Kempston
Hardwick

Biggleswade
Plasmor
Brick
Terminal

Elstow – Redland
Stone Terminal

Wolverton

Transport &
Warehousing
Facilities Ltd.

Forders Sidings
Shanks & McEwan Landfill

Stewartby

BEDFORDSHIRE

BRML
(ZN)

ARC Stone
Terminal

Millbrook

*Ampthill
Tuns.*

CE Tip
Lidlington

Arlesey

Milton Keynes
Central

*Denbigh
Hall
South
Junc.*

Woburn
Sands

Ridgmont

Flitwick

BLETCHLEY

C.S.

BY

Bow Brickhill

Aspley Guise

*Cambridge
Junc.*

CE
Yard

Stone Term.
– Peakstone
and Redland
Roof Tiles

Bletchley

Fenny
Stratford

*Fenny Stratford
Flyover Junc.*

Harlington

CE Plant Depot

Hitchin

LM

WR

*Bletchley
Junc.*

Winslow*

Claydon L.N.E. Junc.
Calvert – Shanks &
McEwan Waste Terminal

Linslade Tuns.

Leighton
Buzzard

*LEIGHTON BUZZARD
N.G. RLY. (2'0")*

Leagrave

Limbury Rd. –
Tarmac Stone T.

Goods & Car Term.

Luton

Grendon Underwood Junc.

Dunstable
(Disused)

*Luton
Bute St*

Quainton Road*

Cheddington

*WHIPSNADE &
UMFOLOZI RLY. (2'6")*

**Akeman Street –
Firmin Coates**

Goods and
Peakstone Terminal

Aylesbury

C.S.

Pitstone (Tring
Cutting) – Castle
Cement Works

*Tring
Summit*

Tring

HERTFORDSHIRE

Harpenden

Stoke
Mandeville

Haddenham &
Thame Parkway

Wendover

*Northchurch
Tuns.*

Berkhamsted

St. Albans
Abbey

St. Albans

Thame –
BP

Little
Kimble

Monks
Risborough

*Dutchlands
Summit*

Hemel
Hempstead

Parcels

Apsley

Park St.

*(SEE MAP
24)*

Chinnor –
Rugby
Cement Works
(Disused)

Princes
Risborough

*Saunderton
Summit*

Great
Missenden

Chesham

King's
Langley

Radlett

Saunderton

(MANTLES
WOOD)

M

LUL

Chalfont
& Latimer

Amersham

WR

Chorley
Wood

Watford

Watford Junc.

BUCKINGHAMSHIRE

Rickmansworth

Croxley
Green

M

Edgware

Stanmore

High Wycombe

Moor
Park

Beaconsfield

Seer Green

(SEE MAP 23)

*Whitehouse
Tun.*

Gerrards
Cross

Denham

Harrow-on-
the-Hill

(SEE MAP 20)

Marlow

Bourne End

Denham Golf
Club

West
Ruislip

M/P

*Rayners
Lane*

C

OXON.

Cookham

Redland
Stone Term.

SLOUGH

Uxbridge

**GREATER
LONDON**

Henley-on-Thames

Furze Platt

Taplow

Burnham

Shell

Slough

*Langley
Total*

Shiplake

BERKSHIRE

Maidenhead

Langley

Iver

West
Drayton

Ealing
Bdy.

C

READING

Wargrave

Windsor & Eton
Central

Datchet

Heathrow

P

Windsor & Eton Riverside

Sunnymeads

(SEE MAP 19)

CE Sidings

Reading

c

Twyford

a) Reading West Junc.
b) Oxford Road Junc.
c) Reading New Junc.

Wraysbury

Feltham

Richmond

RG

a

Reading
West

b

WR

SO

Reading Spur Junc.

C.S.

DL	DOCKLANDS	M	METROPOLITAN
B	BAKERLOO	M(EL)	METROPOLITAN (East London)
C	CENTRAL	N	NORTHERN
O	CIRCLE	P	PICCADILLY
D	DISTRICT	V	VICTORIA
J	JUBILEE		

0   5   10 m.

(1:350,000)

0   5   10   15   km.

Grain Term. – Myhills

● Whittlesford

● Meldreth

CAMBRIDGESHIRE

Duxford
Ciba-Geigy
● Great Chesterford

Dalgetty Franklin
AR
ER
Grain T –
Sherriff
● Royston

1) Willesden Junc.
2) Finsbury Park
3) Stratford
4) Clapham Junction
5) Lewisham
6) London Bridge
7) Victoria
8) Upminster Bridge
9) Hornchurch
10) Elm Park
11) Dagenham East
12) Dagenham Heathway
13) Becontree
14) Upney
a) Tye Green Junc.
b) Coopers Junc.

● Ashwell & Morden

Littlebury Tunnel
Audley End Tunnel

● Audley End

Coal Depot –
Charrington
C.S.
△
● Baldock
● Letchworth
● Letchworth

● Newport

A

● Elsenham *(Summit)*

BP

Stansted North Junc.
Stansted Airport
(To open early 1991)

● Stansed
a
b
Stansted East Junc.
Stansted South Junc.

● Stevenage

HERTFORDSHIRE

Langley
Junc.
Redland Stone Term.

● Knebworth

*Welwyn
North Tun.*
*Welwyn
South Tun.*

Watton-at-Stone
Cory

● Watton-at-Stone

● Welwyn North

● Bishops Stortford

C.S.

Barking Rail
Handling
Services
Transfesa
Depot
RL
C & W
Dagenham
Storage
Car Terminal
Ford
Works

Molewood Tun.

● Ware

C.S.

Freight
Depot
Ripple
Lane Yard
Ripple
Lane FLT
● Dagenham Dock

Welwyn
Garden
City
C.S.
Sidings

● Hertford North
C.S.

● Hertford East

St. Margaret's
E. Austin

● Sawbridgeworth

*(DAGENHAM INSET
FROM BELOW)*

(1:90,000)

Dagenham
Ford Works

● Hatfield

● Bayford

Rye House
Costain

● Roydon

● Harlow Mill

Goods & Foster Yeoman
Stone Terminal

PO Terminal
Redland Stone Terminal

37

● Chelmsford

*Ponsbourne Tun.
(1m. 924yds.)*

● Broxbourne

Broxbourne Junc.
Rye House
Redland Stone Term.

● Harlow Town

ESSEX

Welham
Green

Sidings

● Brookmans Park

● Cuffley

● Cheshunt

North
Weald
Ongar
C

B

Potters
Bar

Epping

● Ingatestone

Theydon Bois
C

● Enfield Town

Debden
C

● Brimsdown

C.S.
Mountnessing Junc.

High
Barnet
Cockfosters
P

N

● Southbury

● Chingford

Woodford
C
Hainault
C

● Shenfield
Ingrave Summit

● Billericay

Mill Hill
East

*(SEE
MAP 25)*

(SEE MAP 26)

GREATER LONDON

C.S.

● Brentwood

Hendon
Central
N

(SEE MAP 21)

Chadwell
Heath

● Romford

CE Sdgs.
Railstore Dist. Dep.

● Harold Wood

● West Horndon

● Laindon
● Basildon

● Hendon

Seven Kings
● Ilford

OLE
Depot

● Gidea Park

Emerson
Pk.

EUL
Depot

● Upminster

2

● Goodmayes

14 13
12
11
10 9 8

● Ockendon

Stanford-le-Hope

C

1

3

M/D

● Barking

*(SEE
INSET ABOVE)*

● Dagenham
Dock

● Rainham

Chafford
Hundred
(Proposed)

Thames Haven Junc.

(SEE INSET P38)

Cliffe
Brett Marine

7

6

North
Woolwich

DL

Abbey
Wood
● Belvedere
● Erith

● Purfleet

● Grays

● East Tilbury

*(SEE
MAP 22)*

● Plumstead
● Welling
Bexleyheath
Slade
Green

Tilbury
Town

Hoo Junc.
Sdgs.

4

5

● Falconwood
● Albany Park
● Sidcup

Barnehurst

● Crayford
Dartford

Tilbury
Riverside

*Hoo
Junc.*

D

● Eltham
● Bexley

● Crayford

● Gravesend
● Higham

*Higham
Tun.*

KENT

Hoo Staff Halt

⬆ 16   ⬆ 17   1   ⬆ 18   10 m.

0
5
(1:350,000)

0   5   10   15   km.

2   DL   DOCKLANDS
B   BAKERLOO
C   CENTRAL
O   CIRCLE
D   DISTRICT
J   JUBILEE

12   M   METROPOLITAN
M(EL) METROPOLITAN (East London)
N   NORTHERN
P   PICCADILLY
V   VICTORIA

36

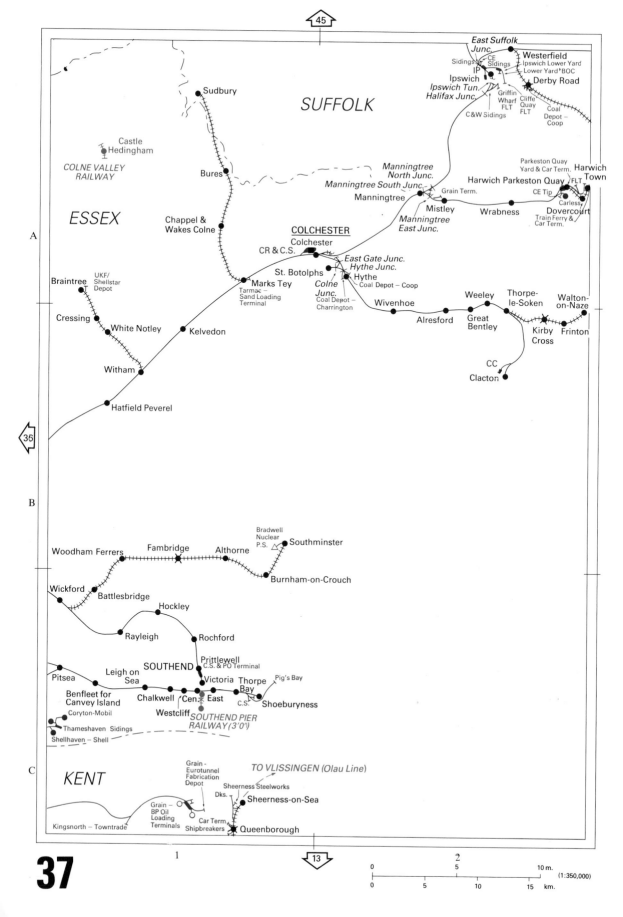

SUFFOLK

East Suffolk Junc.
Westerfield
Sidings IP CE Sidings
Ipswich Lower Yard
Lower Yard BOC
Derby Road
Ipswich
Ipswich Tun.
Halifax Junc.
Griffin Wharf FLT
Cliffe Quay FLT
Coal Depot – Coop
C&W Sidings

Sudbury

Castle Hedingham

COLNE VALLEY RAILWAY

ESSEX

Bures

Chappel & Wakes Colne

Manningtree North Junc.
Manningtree South Junc.
Manningtree
Grain Term.
Mistley
Manningtree East Junc.
Wrabness

Parkeston Quay Yard & Car Term.
Harwich Parkeston Quay
Harwich Town
FLT
CE Tip
Carless
Dovercourt
Train Ferry & Car Term.

A

COLCHESTER
Colchester
CR & C.S.
St. Botolphs
East Gate Junc.
Hythe Junc.
Hythe
Coal Depot – Coop
Colne Junc.
Coal Depot – Charrington

Marks Tey
Tarmac – Sand Loading Terminal

Weeley
Thorpe-le-Soken
Walton-on-Naze

Wivenhoe
Alresford
Great Bentley
Kirby Cross
Frinton

Braintree
UKF/Shellstar Depot

Cressing
White Notley
Kelvedon

Witham

Hatfield Peverel

CC
Clacton

B

Bradwell Nuclear P.S.
Southminster

Woodham Ferrers
Fambridge
Althorne

Burnham-on-Crouch

Wickford
Battlesbridge

Hockley

Rayleigh
Rochford

Prittlewell
C.S. & PO Terminal

SOUTHEND

Leigh on Sea
Victoria
Thorpe Bay
Pig's Bay

Pitsea

Benfleet for Canvey Island
Chalkwell
Cen East
Shoeburyness
C.S.

Coryton-Mobil
Westcliff
SOUTHEND PIER RAILWAY (3'0")

Thameshaven Sidings
Shellhaven – Shell

C

KENT

Grain – Eurotunnel Fabrication Depot

TO VLISSINGEN (Olau Line)

Sheerness Steelworks
Dks.
Sheerness-on-Sea

Grain – BP Oil Loading Terminals

Car Term
Shipbreakers

Kingsnorth – Towntrade

Queenborough

37

1

2

0   5   10 m.
(1:350,000)
0   5   10   15   km.

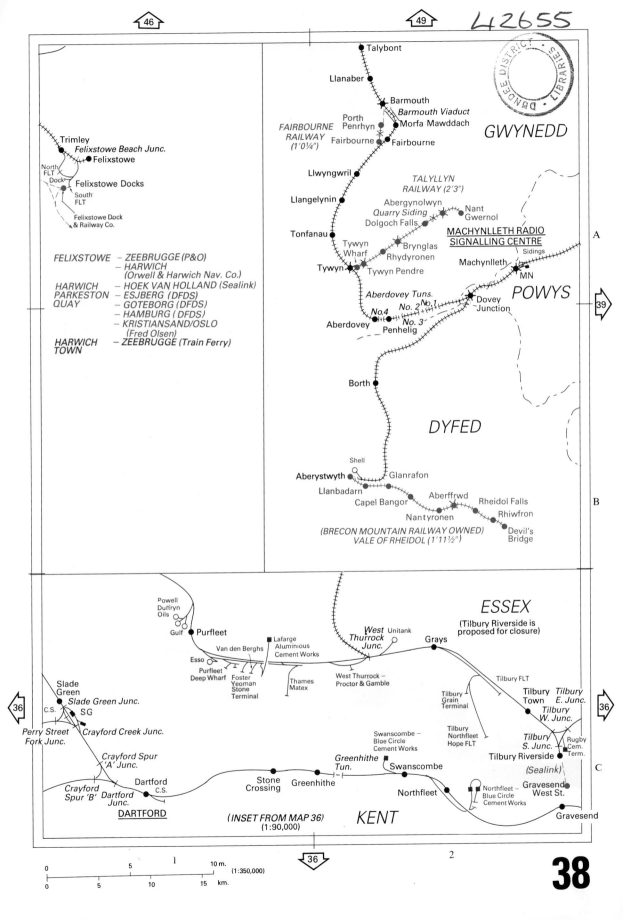

GWYNEDD

POWYS

DYFED

Talybont
Llanaber
Barmouth
Barmouth Viaduct
Porth Penrhyn
Morfa Mawddach
FAIRBOURNE RAILWAY (1'0¼")
Fairbourne
Fairbourne
Llwyngwril
TALYLLYN RAILWAY (2'3")
Llangelynin
Abergynolwyn
Nant Gwernol
Quarry Siding
Dolgoch Falls
Tonfanau
Brynglas
MACHYNLLETH RADIO SIGNALLING CENTRE
Tywyn Wharf
Rhydyronen
Sidings
Tywyn
Tywyn Pendre
Machynlleth
MN
Aberdovey Tuns.
No.4 No.2 No.1
No.3
Dovey Junction
Aberdovey
Penhelig
Borth

Shell
Aberystwyth
Glanrafon
Llanbadarn
Aberffrwd
Rheidol Falls
Capel Bangor
Nantyronen
Rhiwfron
Devil's Bridge
(BRECON MOUNTAIN RAILWAY OWNED)
VALE OF RHEIDOL (1'11½")

Trimley
Felixstowe Beach Junc.
Felixstowe
North FLT Dock
Felixstowe Docks
South FLT
Felixstowe Dock & Railway Co.

FELIXSTOWE – ZEEBRUGGE (P&O)
– HARWICH (Orwell & Harwich Nav. Co.)
HARWICH – HOEK VAN HOLLAND (Sealink)
PARKESTON – ESJBERG (DFDS)
QUAY – GOTEBORG (DFDS)
– HAMBURG (DFDS)
– KRISTIANSAND/OSLO (Fred Olsen)
HARWICH – ZEEBRUGGE (Train Ferry)
TOWN

ESSEX
(Tilbury Riverside is proposed for closure)

Powell Duffryn Oils
Gulf
Purfleet
Van den Berghs
Lafarge Aluminious Cement Works
West Thurrock Junc.
Unitank
Grays
Esso
Purfleet Deep Wharf
Foster Yeoman Stone Terminal
Thames Matex
West Thurrock – Proctor & Gamble
Tilbury FLT
Tilbury Grain Terminal
Tilbury Town
Tilbury E. Junc.
Tilbury Northfleet Hope FLT
Tilbury W. Junc.
Swanscombe – Blue Circle Cement Works
Tilbury S. Junc.
Rugby Cem. Term.
Tilbury Riverside
Slade Green
Slade Green Junc.
C.S.   SG
Perry Street Fork Junc.
Crayford Creek Junc.
Crayford Spur 'A' Junc.
Dartford C.S.
Greenhithe Tun.
Greenhithe
Swanscombe
(Sealink)
Gravesend West St.
Crayford Spur 'B'
Dartford Junc.
DARTFORD
Stone Crossing
Greenhithe
Northfleet
Northfleet – Blue Circle Cement Works
Gravesend

(INSET FROM MAP 36)
(1:90,000)
KENT

36   36   39

0   5   1   10 m.
(1:350,000)
0   5   10   15   km.

36

38

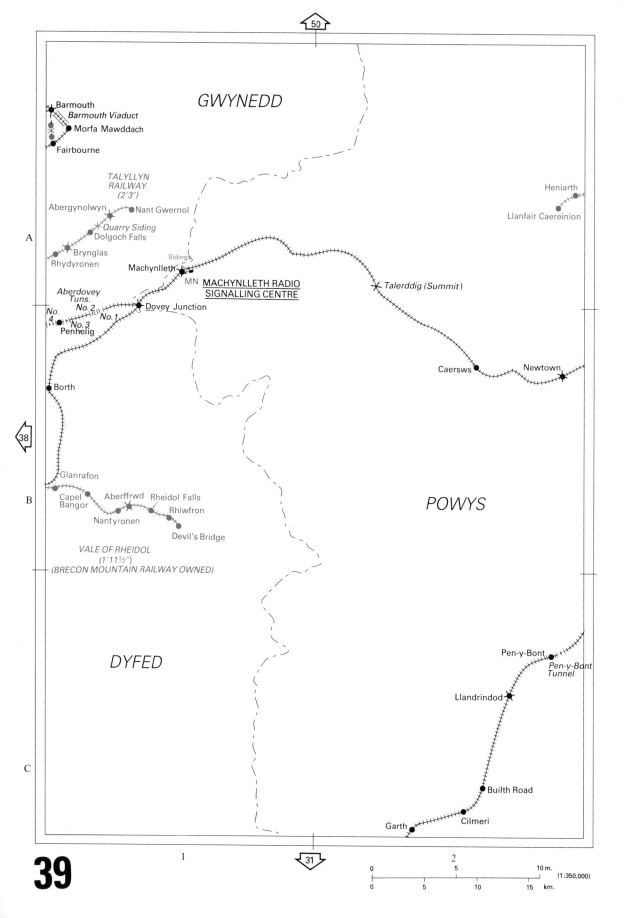

GWYNEDD

Barmouth
Barmouth Viaduct
Morfa Mawddach
Fairbourne

*TALYLLYN
RAILWAY
(2'3")*

Heniarth
Llanfair Caereinion

Abergynolwyn   Nant Gwernol
Quarry Siding
Dolgoch Falls
A
Brynglas
Rhydyronen
Siddings
Machynlleth
MN   MACHYNLLETH RADIO
SIGNALLING CENTRE

Talerddig (Summit)

*Aberdovey
Tuns.*
No.   No. 2
4   No. 1
Dovey Junction
No. 3
Penhelig

Caersws   Newtown

38

Borth

Glanrafon
B
Capel
Bangor   Aberffrwd   Rheidol Falls
Rhiwfron
Nantyronen
Devil's Bridge

POWYS

*VALE OF RHEIDOL
(1'11½")*
(BRECON MOUNTAIN RAILWAY OWNED)

Pen-y-Bont
*Pen-y-Bont
Tunnel*

DYFED

Llandrindod

C

Builth Road

Garth   Cilmeri

39

1   2

0   5   10 m.
0   5   10   15   km.
(1:350,000)

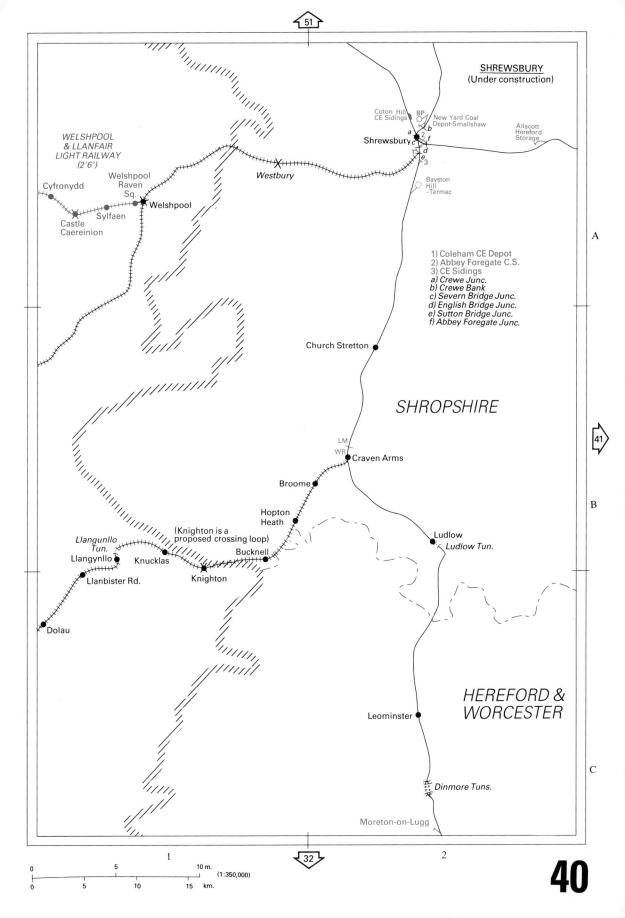

SHREWSBURY
(Under construction)

Coton Hill
CE Sidings
BP
New Yard Coal
Depot-Smallshaw
Allscott
Hereford
Storage

a *b*
Shrewsbury
2 *f*
c
1 *d*
e
3

Bayston
Hill
-Tarmac

*WELSHPOOL
& LLANFAIR
LIGHT RAILWAY
(2'6")*

Cyfronydd

Welshpool
Raven
Sq.

Westbury

Sylfaen
Welshpool

Castle
Caereinion

A

1) Coleham CE Depot
2) Abbey Foregate C.S.
3) CE Sidings
a) Crewe Junc.
b) Crewe Bank
c) Severn Bridge Junc.
d) English Bridge Junc.
e) Sutton Bridge Junc.
f) Abbey Foregate Junc.

Church Stretton

SHROPSHIRE

LM
WR
Craven Arms

Broome

B

Hopton
Heath

Ludlow
Ludlow Tun.

*Llangunllo
Tun.*

(Knighton is a
proposed crossing loop)

Bucknell

Llangynllo
Knucklas

Llanbister Rd.
Knighton

Dolau

*HEREFORD &
WORCESTER*

Leominster

C

Dinmore Tuns.

Moreton-on-Lugg

1

2

0   5   10 m.

(1:350,000)

0   5   10   15   km.

40

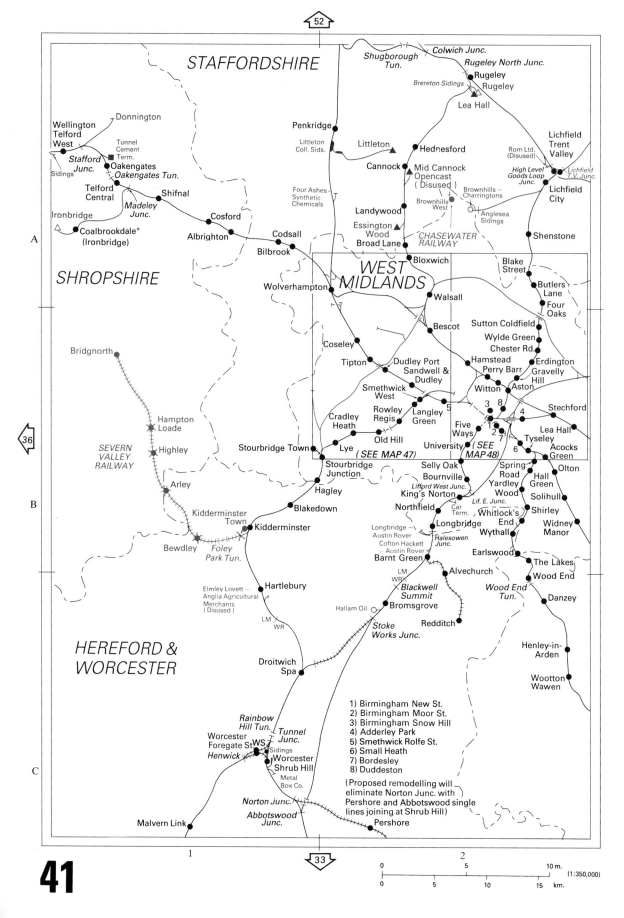

STAFFORDSHIRE

Shugborough Tun.

Colwich Junc.

Rugeley North Junc.

Brereton Sidings Rugeley Rugeley

Lea Hall

Penkridge

Littleton Coll. Sids. Littleton Hednesford

Wellington
Telford West

Donnington

Tunnel Cement Term. Oakengates
Stafford Junc. *Oakengates Tun.*

Sidings

Telford Central Shifnal

Madeley Junc.

Cannock Mid Cannock Opencast (Disused)

Landywood

Four Ashes – Synthetic Chemicals

Rom Ltd. (Disused)
High Level Goods Loop Junc.

Lichfield Trent Valley

Lichfield T.V. Junc.

Lichfield City

Ironbridge Coalbrookdale* (Ironbridge)

Albrighton

Cosford

Codsall

Essington Wood Brownhills – Charringtons
Broad Lane Brownhills West
CHASEWATER RAILWAY

Anglesea Sidings

Shenstone

SHROPSHIRE

Bilbrook

Wolverhampton

Bloxwich

WEST MIDLANDS

Walsall

Blake Street

Butlers Lane

Four Oaks

A

Bescot

Sutton Coldfield

Wylde Green

Chester Rd.

Coseley

Tipton

Dudley Port
Sandwell & Dudley

Hamstead
Perry Barr

Erdington
Gravelly Hill

Bridgnorth

Smethwick West

Witton Aston

Stechford

SEVERN VALLEY RAILWAY

Hampton Loade

Highley

Cradley Heath

Rowley Regis Langley Green

3 8

1

4

Lea Hall

36

Arley

Stourbridge Town

Lye

Old Hill

Five Ways

2 7

Tyseley

Acocks Green

University

(SEE MAP 47)

(SEE MAP 48)

6

Olton

B

Kidderminster Town

Bewdley

Foley Park Tun.

Kidderminster

Hagley

Blakedown

Stourbridge Junction

Selly Oak
Bournville

King's Norton
Lifford West Junc.

Northfield

Lif. E. Junc.

Spring Road
Yardley Wood

Hall Green

Solihull

Shirley

Whitlock's End

Widney Manor

Hartlebury

Elmley Lovett – Anglia Agricultural Merchants (Disused)

Longbridge – Austin Rover
Cofton Hackett – Austin Rover
Halesowen Junc.

Longbridge

Wythall

Car Term.

Earlswood

The Lakes

Wood End

HEREFORD & WORCESTER

LM WR

Hallam Oil

Barnt Green

LM
WR

Blackwell Summit

Bromsgrove

Alvechurch

Wood End Tun.

Danzey

Redditch

Droitwich Spa

Stoke Works Junc.

Henley-in-Arden

Wootton Wawen

C

Rainbow Hill Tun.

Worcester Foregate St. WS
Henwick

Tunnel Junc.

Sidings

Worcester Shrub Hill

Metal Box Co.

1) Birmingham New St.
2) Birmingham Moor St.
3) Birmingham Snow Hill
4) Adderley Park
5) Smethwick Rolfe St.
6) Small Heath
7) Bordesley
8) Duddeston

(Proposed remodelling will eliminate Norton Junc. with Pershore and Abbotswood single lines joining at Shrub Hill)

Malvern Link

Norton Junc.

Abbotswood Junc.

Pershore

41

1 2

0 5 10 m.

(1:350,000)

0 5 10 15 km.

DERBYSHIRE

Drakelow

Castle Gresley
(Projected)

Rawdon

*Wichnor
Junc.*

Lounge Opencast
D.P.

*Moira
West
Junc.*

Moira
(Projected)

*Lounge
Junc.*

Swannington
(Projected)

Ashby-
de-la-
Zouch

Mantle Lane Sidings
(Coalville)

Coalville
Loco H.S.

Coalville
(Projected)

Marcroft Wagon
Repair Wks.

Bardon Hill – Prismo Bitumen

Bardon Hill Quarries

Cliffe Hill – Tarmac (Disused)

Stud Farm –
Tarmac

Coalfield
Farm

(Projected new stations for
Loughborough – Leicester –
Coalville – Burton – Derby
service)

*Bagworth Colliery
Junc. (Ellistown)*

Bagworth
(Projected)

Bagworth

Shackerstone

BATTLEFIELD
LINE

(Proposed
extension)

Market
Bosworth

Shenton

Brush Works –
Stone Term. – ARC

Loughborough
Loughborough Chord Junc.

Loughborough
Central

Barrow
upon Soar
(Projected)

Quorn &
Woodhouse

Mountsorrel
(Redland Roadstone –
Barrow-upon-Soar)

Sileby
(Projected)

GREAT
CENTRAL
RAILWAY

Rothley

Belgrave
& Birstall

(Under
construction)

N.   E.
Syston Juncs.
Syston
(Projected)
S.

Nedham
St.Goods

Braunstone Gate –
Berry & Piggott Scrapyards

Humberstone Rd.

LR

Leicester

Parcels

LEICESTER   A

Desford
(Projected)

Kirkby
Muxloe
(Projected)

1   2

3

Knighton Tun.

Leicester Forest
East (Projected)

Saffron Lane
(Disused)

Knighton South Junc.

Glen Parva Junc.

N. Wigston
Sidings
Wigston Juncs.

Narborough

South
Wigston

S.

Croft –
ECC Quarries

Tamworth

Polesworth

LEICESTERSHIRE

Wilnecote

*Kibworth
Summit*

Atherstone

1) Park Rise (Projected)
2) Ainsdale Road (Projected)
3) Bede Island (Projected)

Kingsbury
(Proposed)

Kingsbury – Warwickshire Oil
Scrapyard – G. Cohen

Hartshill
Tarmac

*Nuneaton
North
Junc.*

NUNEATON

Hinckley

*Water
Orton E.
Junc.*

*Kingsbury
Junc.*

*Whitacre
Junc.*

Daw Mill
(Whitacre)

Abbey Junc.

Nuneaton

Midland Junc.

Hams Hall
(Disused)

*Arley
Tun.*

*Nuneaton
South Junc.*

Water
Orton

Marston
Green

Bedworth
(Proposed)

Bedworth –
Murco

Birmingham
International

Hampton-
in-Arden

Coventry Coll.
(Keresley)

Coventry Homefire
Coking Plant

Sidings

Birmingham
Airport
Maglev
Link

Hawkhurst
Moor
(Projected)

*Three
Spires
Junc.*

Tile
Hill

*Trent
Valley
Junc.*

Grundig
Warehouse
Engineers'
Sidings

B

Berkswell

*Beechwood
Tun.*

Canley

New Bilton
Rugby Cement Works &
Redland Roof Tiles

Rugby

Coventry

RUGBY

Dorridge

COVENTRY

Crick. Tun.

Watford Lodge Tun.

Lapworth

(Projected
new rly.)

Kenilworth

*Kilsby
Tunnel
(1m 666yds)*

Long
Buckby

*Hatton
N. Junc.*
Hatton

*Hatton W.
Junc.*

*Hatton
Station
Junc.*

Leamington
Spa

WARWICKSHIRE

Claverdon

Warwick

*Stowe
Hill
Tunnel*

LEAMINGTON SPA

Bearley

Bearley Junc.

Greaves Sidings

Wilmcote

Harbury –
Blue Circle Cem Wks.

Stratford-
upon-Avon

NORTHAMPTONSHIRE   C

Fenny Compton

LM   WR

Kineton

1

2

0   5   10 m.

(1:350,000)

0   5   10   15   km.

42

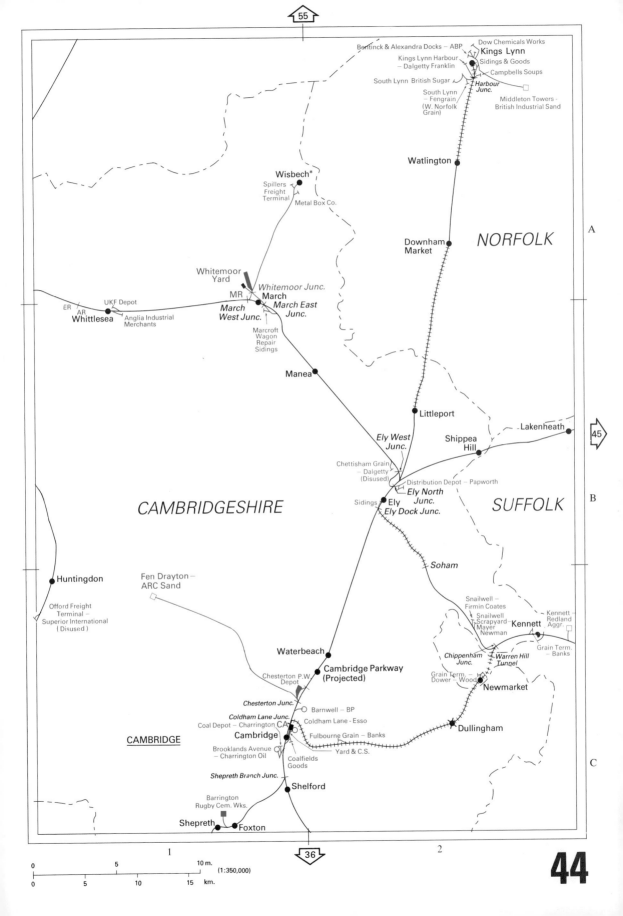

Bentinck & Alexandra Docks – ABP
Dow Chemicals Works
Kings Lynn Harbour – Dalgetty Franklin
Kings Lynn
Sidings & Goods
Campbells Soups
South Lynn British Sugar
Harbour Junc.
South Lynn – Fengrain (W. Norfolk Grain)
Middleton Towers – British Industrial Sand

Watlington

Wisbech*
Spillers Freight Terminal
Metal Box Co.

NORFOLK

Downham Market

Whitemoor Yard
Whitemoor Junc.
MR
March
March East Junc.
ER AR UKF Depot
March West Junc.
Whittlesea
Anglia Industrial Merchants
Marcroft Wagon Repair Sidings

Manea

Littleport

Lakenheath

Ely West Junc.
Shippea Hill

Chettisham Grain – Dalgetty (Disused)
Distribution Depot – Papworth
Ely North Junc.

CAMBRIDGESHIRE

Sidings **Ely**
Ely Dock Junc.

SUFFOLK

Soham

Huntingdon

Fen Drayton – ARC Sand

Offord Freight Terminal – Superior International (Disused)

Snailwell – Firmin Coates
Snailwell Scrapyard – Mayer Newman
Kennett – Redland Aggr.
Kennett
Grain Term. – Banks

Waterbeach

Cambridge Parkway (Projected)
Chippenham Junc.
Warren Hill Tunnel

Chesterton P.W. Depot

Grain Term. – Dower – Wood
Newmarket

Chesterton Junc.
Barnwell – BP
Coldham Lane Junc.
Coldham Lane – Esso
Coal Depot – Charrington CA
Cambridge
Fulbourne Grain – Banks
Yard & C.S.
Dullingham

CAMBRIDGE
Brooklands Avenue – Charrington Oil
Coalfields Goods

Shepreth Branch Junc.
Shelford

Barrington Rugby Cem. Wks.
Shepreth Foxton

0   5   10 m.   (1:350,000)
0   5   10   15   km.

44

A

B

C

45

1   2

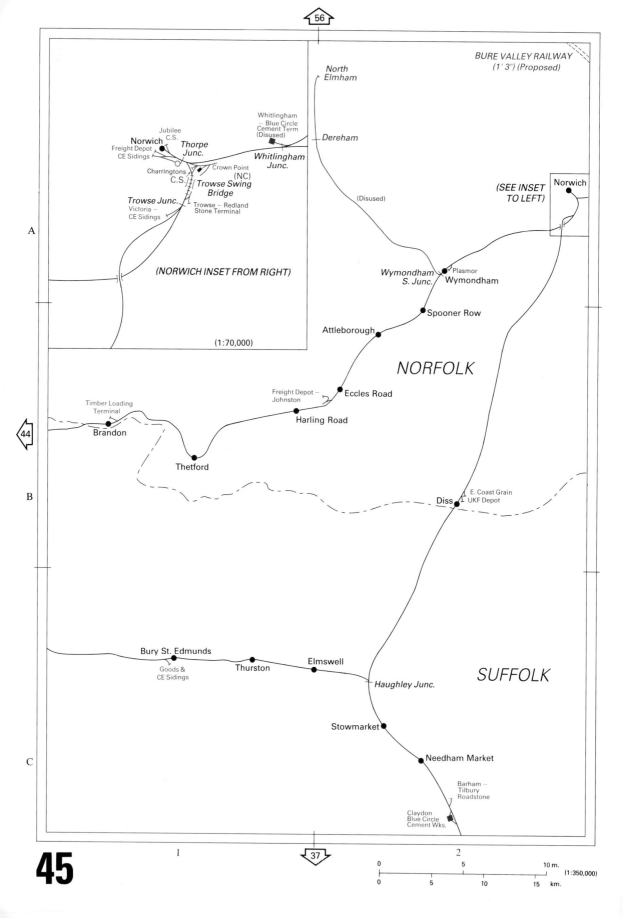

BURE VALLEY RAILWAY
(1' 3") (Proposed)

North
Elmham

Whitlingham
– Blue Circle
Cement Term.
(Disused)

Jubilee
C.S.
Norwich
Freight Depot
CE Sidings   *Thorpe*
Junc.
Charringtons   Crown Point
C.S.   (NC)
Trowse Swing
Bridge
Trowse Junc.
Victoria –
CE Sidings   Trowse – Redland
Stone Terminal

Dereham

Whitlingham
Junc.

(Disused)

Norwich

(SEE INSET
TO LEFT)

A

(NORWICH INSET FROM RIGHT)

Plasmor
Wymondham
S. Junc.   Wymondham

Spooner Row

(1:70,000)

Attleborough

NORFOLK

Timber Loading
Terminal

Freight Depot –
Johnston   Eccles Road

Brandon

Harling Road

44

E. Coast Grain
UKF Depot

B   Diss

Thetford

Bury St. Edmunds

Goods &
CE Sidings   Thurston   Elmswell

SUFFOLK

Haughley Junc.

Stowmarket

Needham Market

C

Barham –
Tilbury
Roadstone

Claydon
Blue Circle
Cement Wks.

45

1

2

0   5   10 m.

(1:350,000)

0   5   10   15   km.

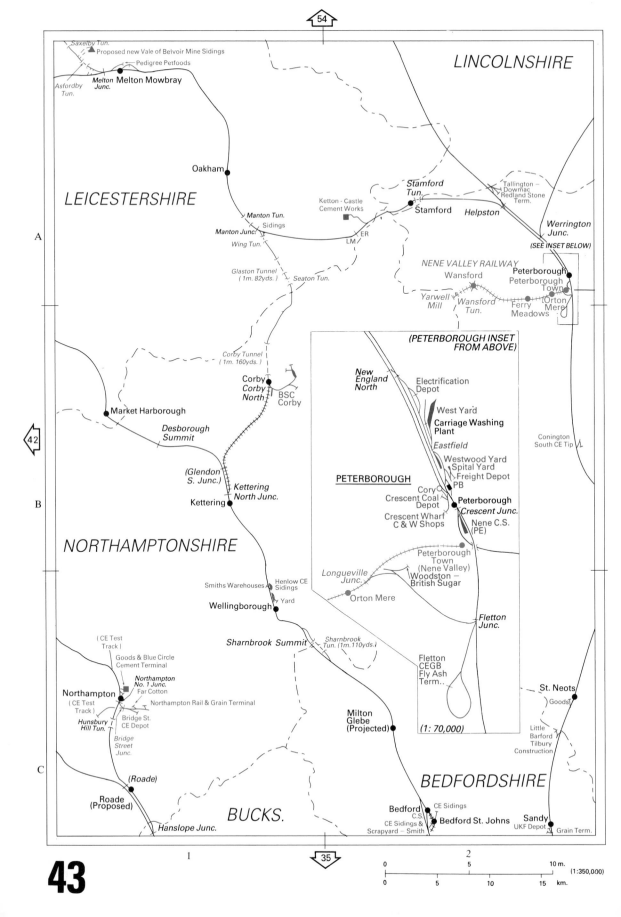

LINCOLNSHIRE

Saxelby Tun.
▲ Proposed new Vale of Belvoir Mine Sidings
— Pedigree Petfoods
Melton Melton Mowbray
Asfordby *Junc.*
Tun.

LEICESTERSHIRE

Oakham

Stamford Tun.
Ketton – Castle
Cement Works ■
Manton Tun. Sidings
Manton Junc.
Wing Tun.
ER
LM
Stamford   *Helpston*

Tallington –
Dowmac
Redland Stone
Term.

Werrington Junc.
(SEE INSET BELOW)

A

Glaston Tunnel
(1m. 82yds.)   *Seaton Tun.*

NENE VALLEY RAILWAY
Wansford
Yarwell *Wansford*
Mill *Tun.*
Ferry
Meadows

Peterborough
Peterborough
Town
Orton
Mere

(PETERBOROUGH INSET
FROM ABOVE)

Corby Tunnel
(1m. 160yds.)

New
England
North

Electrification
Depot

West Yard
Carriage Washing
Plant
Eastfield

Corby
Corby
North
BSC
Corby

Market Harborough

Desborough
Summit

(Glendon
S. Junc.)

Kettering
North Junc.
Kettering

PETERBOROUGH

Westwood Yard
Spital Yard
Freight Depot
PB
Cory
Crescent Coal
Depot
Crescent Wharf
C & W Shops
Peterborough
Crescent Junc.
Nene C.S.
(PE)

Conington
South CE Tip

B

NORTHAMPTONSHIRE

Smiths Warehouses ▲
Henlow CE
Sidings
Yard
Wellingborough

Longueville
Junc.
Orton Mere

Peterborough
Town
(Nene Valley)
Woodston –
British Sugar

Fletton
Junc.

Sharnbrook Summit
Sharnbrook
Tun. (1m.110yds.)

Fletton
CEGB
Fly Ash
Term..

(CE Test
Track)
Goods & Blue Circle
Cement Terminal
Northampton
No. 1 Junc.
Far Cotton
Northampton
(CE Test
Track)
Northampton Rail & Grain Terminal
Hunsbury
Hill Tun.
Bridge St.
CE Depot
Bridge
Street
Junc.

Milton
Glebe
(Projected)

(1: 70,000)

St. Neots
Goods

Little
Barford
Tilbury
Construction

C

(Roade)
Roade
(Proposed)

Hanslope Junc.

BUCKS.

BEDFORDSHIRE

Bedford
C.S.
CE Sidings &
Scrapyard – Smith
CE Sidings
Bedford St. Johns

Sandy
UKF Depot
Grain Term.

43

1   2

0   5   10 m.
0   5   10   15   km.
(1:350,000)

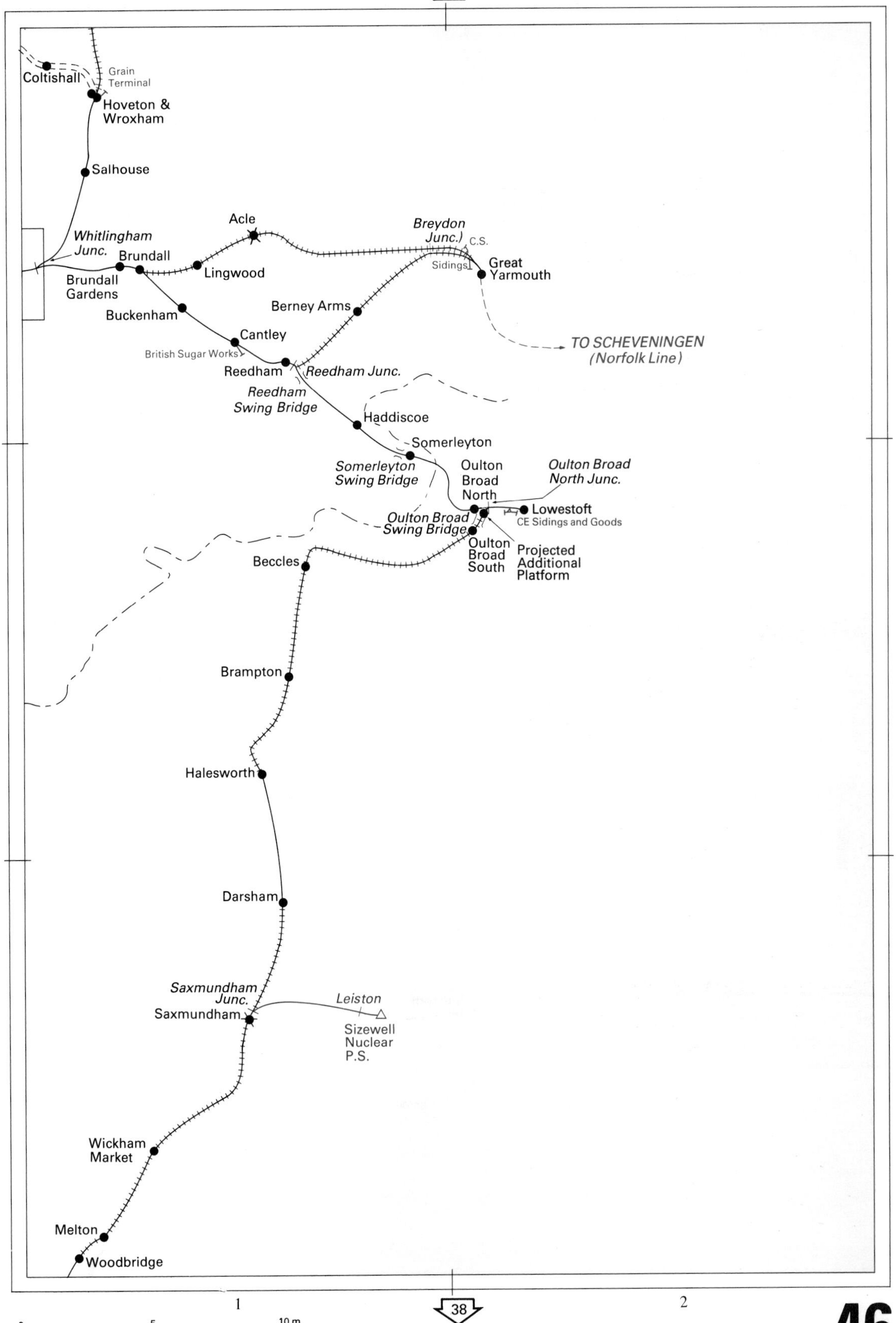

Coltishall

Grain Terminal

Hoveton & Wroxham

Salhouse

Acle

Breydon Junc.) C.S.

Whitlingham Junc. Brundall

Lingwood

Sidings

Great Yarmouth

Brundall Gardens

Buckenham

Berney Arms

Cantley

British Sugar Works

Reedham *Reedham Junc.*

Reedham Swing Bridge

Haddiscoe

Somerleyton

Somerleyton Swing Bridge

Oulton Broad North

Oulton Broad North Junc.

Oulton Broad Swing Bridge

Lowestoft
CE Sidings and Goods

Oulton Broad South

Projected Additional Platform

TO SCHEVENINGEN (Norfolk Line)

A

Beccles

Brampton

Halesworth

B

Darsham

Saxmundham Junc.

Saxmundham

Leiston

Sizewell Nuclear P.S.

Wickham Market

C

Melton

Woodbridge

1

2

0   5   10 m.
(1:350,000)

0   5   10   15   km.

46

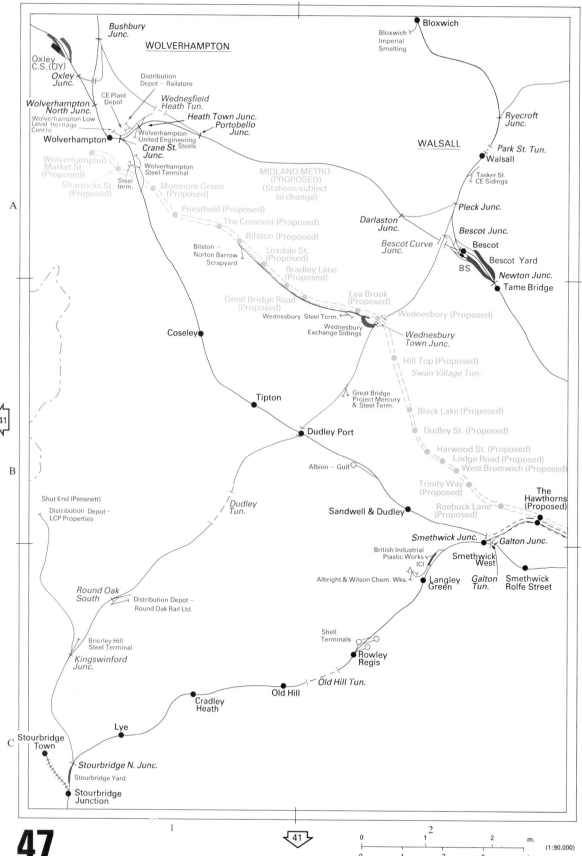

Bloxwich

Bloxwich Imperial Smelting

Bushbury Junc.

WOLVERHAMPTON

Oxley C.S. (OY)

Oxley Junc.

Ryecroft Junc.

Distribution Depot – Railstore

Wednesfield Heath Tun.

CE Plant Depot

Wolverhampton North Junc.

Wolverhampton Low Level Heritage Centre

Heath Town Junc.

Portobello Junc.

WALSALL

Park St. Tun.

Walsall

Wolverhampton

Wolverhampton United Engineering Steels

Crane St. Junc.

Tasker St. CE Sidings

Wolverhampton Market St. (Proposed)

Wolverhampton Steel Terminal

Steel term.

Pleck Junc.

Sharrocks St. (Proposed)

Monmore Green (Proposed)

MIDLAND METRO (PROPOSED) (Stations subject to change)

Darlaston Junc.

Bescot Junc.

Priestfield (Proposed)

Bescot

The Crescent (Proposed)

Bescot Curve Junc.

Bescot Yard

Bilston (Proposed)

BS

Bilston – Norton Barrow Scrapyard

Loxdale St. (Proposed)

Newton Junc.

Tame Bridge

Bradley Lane (Proposed)

Lea Brook (Proposed)

Great Bridge Road (Proposed)

Wednesbury (Proposed)

Coseley

Wednesbury Steel Term.

Wednesbury Exchange Sidings

Wednesbury Town Junc.

Hill Top (Proposed)

Swan Village Tun.

Tipton

Great Bridge Project Mercury & Steel Term.

Black Lake (Proposed)

Dudley Port

Dudley St. (Proposed)

Albion – Gulf

Harwood St. (Proposed)

Lodge Road (Proposed)

West Bromwich (Proposed)

Shut End (Pensnett)

Distribution Depot– LCP Properties

Dudley Tun.

Trinity Way (Proposed)

The Hawthorns (Proposed)

Sandwell & Dudley

Roebuck Lane (Proposed)

Smethwick Junc.

Galton Junc.

Round Oak South

British Industrial Plastic Works

ICI

Smethwick West

Galton Tun.

Smethwick Rolfe Street

Distribution Depot – Round Oak Rail Ltd.

Albright & Wilson Chem. Wks.

Langley Green

Brierley Hill Steel Terminal

Kingswinford Junc.

Shell Terminals

Rowley Regis

Cradley Heath

Old Hill

Old Hill Tun.

Lye

Stourbridge Town

Stourbridge N. Junc.

Stourbridge Yard

Stourbridge Junction

47

0   1   2   m.

(1:90,000)

0   1   2   3   4 km.

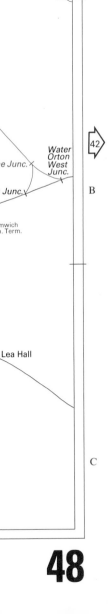

STAFFORDSHIRE

WARWICKS.

WEST
MIDLANDS

Blake
Street

Butlers
Lane

Four
Oaks
C.S.

A

Sutton Park
CE Sidings

Sutton Coldfield *Sutton Coldfield Tun.*

Wylde
Green

Chester
Road

Hamstead

Erdington

Water
Orton
West
Junc.

42

*Perry Barr
North Junc.*

Park Lane Junc.

*Perry Barr
West Junc.*

*Perry Barr
South Junc.*

Imperial
Metal Wks.

Gravelly Hill

*Castle
Bromwich Junc.*

B

Perry
Barr

Witton

Stone
Terminal

Castle Bromwich
– MEB

Castle Bromwich
Castle Cem. Term.

*Hamstead
Tun.*

Booth St.
(Proposed)

Handsworth &
Smethwick
Blue Circle
Cem. Term.

Aston

BSC
Bromford

Bromford
Bridge – Esso

Coopers
Scrapyd.

Handsworth (Proposed)

Washwood
Heath Yard

RMC Stone Terminal

*E.
S.* Sl

Benson Rd. (Proposed)

All Saints (Proposed)

C & W
Shops

Metro – Cammell
Carriage Works

*N.
Soho
Juncs.*

Jewellery Quarter (Proposed)

SALTLEY

*(Proposed
Railway)*

Duddeston

Tunnels

Lawley St. FLT

Stechford

Ladywood
(Projected)

Birmingham
Snow Hill

Curzon St. –
Castle Cem.
Term.

Sidings

Landor St. Junc.

Adderley Park

SY

Lea Hall

*Snow
Hill
Tun.*

New Street North Tun.

Birmingham
New St.

*Holliday St. Tun.
Canal Tun.*

Proof
House
Junc.

Grand
Junc.

St. Andrews Junc.

NEW ST.

Granville St. Tun.

Bath Row Tun.

*New St.
Sth. Tun.*

Bordesley

Bordesley Junc.

Five Ways

*Suffolk St.
Tun.*

Birmingham
Moor St.

Bordesley Car
Terminal – MAT

Small Heath
Small Heath South Junc.

*Church
Road Tun.*

Small Heath
Coal Depot
LCP Fuels

Norton Persto
Scrapyard

DMU & C.S.

Car Term. – Tolemans

C

University

TS

Standard Gauge
Steam Trust

Tyseley
Tyseley South Junc.

Acocks Green

Allen
Rowland
Works

Moseley Tun.

0   1   2   m.

(1:90,000)

0   1   2   3   4 km.

48

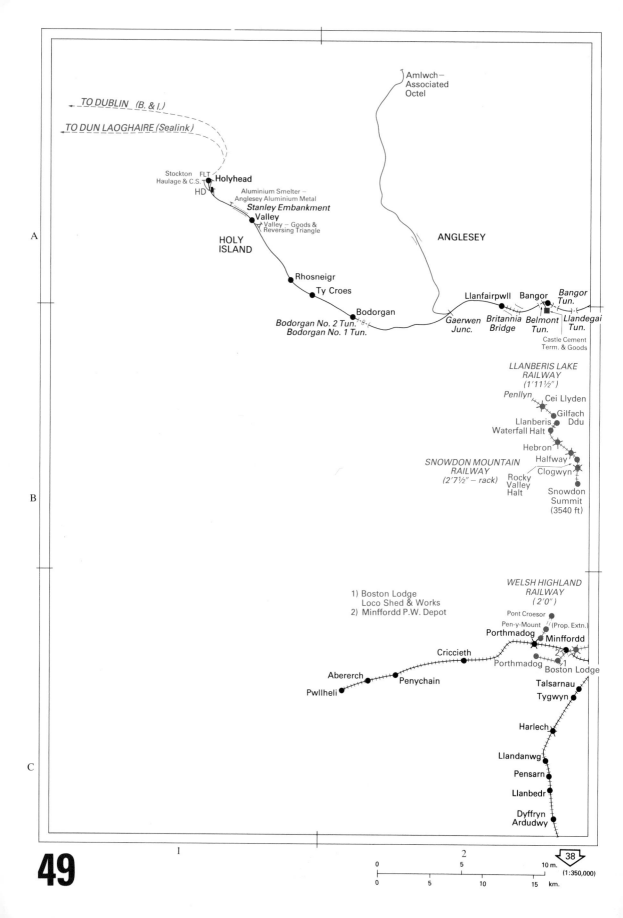

TO DUBLIN (B. & I.)

TO DUN LAOGHAIRE (Sealink)

Amlwch –
Associated
Octel

Stockton FLT **Holyhead**
Haulage & C.S.
HD
Aluminium Smelter –
Anglesey Aluminium Metal
Stanley Embankment
Valley
Valley – Goods &
Reversing Triangle

ANGLESEY

A

**HOLY
ISLAND**

Rhosneigr
Ty Croes

Bodorgan

Bodorgan No. 2 Tun.
Bodorgan No. 1 Tun.

Llanfairpwll **Bangor** *Bangor
Tun.*

Gaerwen *Britannia* *Belmont* *Llandegai*
Junc. *Bridge* *Tun.* *Tun.*

Castle Cement
Term. & Goods

*LLANBERIS LAKE
RAILWAY*
(1'11½")

Penllyn Cei Llyden
Gilfach
Llanberis Ddu
Waterfall Halt
Hebron
SNOWDON MOUNTAIN Halfway
RAILWAY Clogwyn
(2'7½" – rack) Rocky
Valley
Halt Snowdon
Summit
(3540 ft)

B

*WELSH HIGHLAND
RAILWAY
(2'0")*

Pont Croesor
Pen-y-Mount (Prop. Extn.)
Porthmadog
Minffordd

1) Boston Lodge
Loco Shed & Works
2) Minffordd P.W. Depot

Porthmadog
Boston Lodge

Criccieth

Abererch
Penychain
Pwllheli

Talsarnau
Tygwyn

Harlech

Llandanwg
Pensarn
Llanbedr

**Dyffryn
Ardudwy**

C

49

1

2

38

0 10 m.
(1:350,000)
0 5
0 5 10 15 km.

GREAT ORME TRAMWAY
(ABERCONWY DISTRICT COUNCIL)
(3' 6")

Great Orme
Halfway
Llandudno Victoria
Llandudno

Point of Ayr
Talacre
Prestatyn

Conwy Tubular Bridge
C.S.
Deganwy
Rhyl

*Penmaenbach
Tun.*
Penmaenmawr
ARC
LJ
Colwyn Bay
*Penmaenrhos
Tun.*
Abergele &
Pensarn

*Penclip
Tun.*
Conwy Morfa
– Welsh Office
Llandudno Junc.

Conwy
Penmaenmawr
Goods, Heron Oil &
Blue Circle Cem. Term.

Llanfairfechan
Glan Conwy

Tal-y-Cafn

Dolgarrog

CLWYD

Llanrwst North
Llanrwst

51

Betws-y-Coed

Pont-y-Pant
*Beaverpool
Tun.*

*Pont-y-Pant
Upper Tun.*
*Pont-y-Pant
Lower Tun.*
Dolwyddelan
Roman Bridge

*FFESTINIOG
RAILWAY
(1'11½")*
*Ffestiniog Tunnel
(2m. 338yds.)*

Glan-y-Pwll
Depot
Tan-y-Grisiau
Blaenau Ffestiniog

Moelwyn Tun.
Tan-y-Bwlch
Dduallt
Campbells
Platform
Rhiw Goch
Plas Halt
Penrhyn
Penrhyndeudraeth
Maentwrog Road *

Llandecwyn
Trawsfynydd
Nuclear P.S.

GWYNEDD

Bala
Golf Club Halt
Bryn Hynod
Glan Llyn Halt
Llangywair
Pentrepiod Halt
*BALA LAKE
RAILWAY
(1'11½")*
Llanuwchllyn

C

POWYS

2

39

0   5   10 m.
                    (1:350,000)
0   5   10   15 km.

50

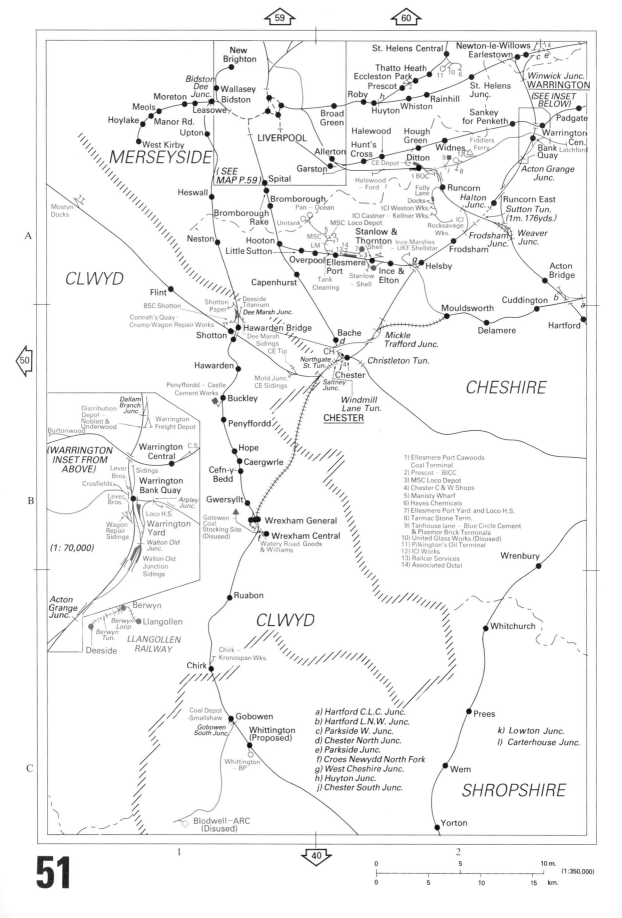

New Brighton
Bidston Dee Junc.
Wallasey
Moreton
Bidston
Leasowe
Meols
Upton
Hoylake
Manor Rd.
West Kirby

MERSEYSIDE

St. Helens Central
Thatto Heath
Eccleston Park
Prescot
Roby
Huyton
Rainhill
Whiston
Broad Green

Newton-le-Willows
Earlestown
Winwick Junc.
WARRINGTON
(SEE INSET BELOW)
St. Helens Junc.
Sankey for Penketh
Padgate
Warrington Cen.
Bank Quay
Latchford
Acton Grange Junc.

LIVERPOOL
(SEE MAP P.59)
Spital

Halewood
Hunt's Cross
Allerton
Garston
Widnes
Hough Green
Fiddlers Ferry
Ditton
CE Depot
(BOC)
Halewood – Ford
Folly Lane Wks.
Runcorn
Halton Junc.
Runcorn East
Sutton Tun.
(1m. 176yds.)

CLWYD

Heswall
Bromborough
Pan – Ocean
Unitank
Bromborough Rake
Neston
Hooton
Little Sutton
Overpool
Ellesmere Port
Capenhurst
Tank Cleaning
ICI Weston Wks.
MSC Loco Depot
MSC LM
Stanlow & Thornton
Shell
Ince Marshes – UKF Shellstar
Stanlow – Shell
Ince & Elton
Helsby
ICI Castner – Kellner Wks.
ICI Rocksavage Wks.
Frodsham Junc.
Frodsham
Weaver Junc.
Acton Bridge
Mostyn Docks

Mouldsworth
Cuddington
Delamere
Hartford

Flint
BSC Shotton
Deeside Titanium
Shotton Paper
Dee Marsh Junc.
Connah's Quay – Crump Wagon Repair Works
Shotton
Hawarden Bridge
Dee Marsh Sidings
CE Tip
Bache
CH
Mickle Trafford Junc.
Northgate St. Tun.
Christleton Tun.
Chester
Saltney Junc.
Mold Junc.
CE Sidings
Windmill Lane Tun.
CHESTER

CHESHIRE

Hawarden
Penyffordd – Castle Cement Works
Buckley
Penyffordd
Hope
Caergwrle
Cefn-y-Bedd
Gwersyllt

Distribution Depot – Noblett & Underwood
Dallam Branch Junc.
Warrington Freight Depot
Burtonwood
(WARRINGTON INSET FROM ABOVE)
Warrington Central
C.S.
Lever Bros.
Sidings
Crosfields
Lever Bros.
Warrington Bank Quay
Arpley Junc.
Loco H.S.
Wagon Repair Sidings
Warrington Yard
Walton Old Junc.
Walton Old Junction Sidings
(1: 70,000)

Gatewen Coal Stocking Site (Disused)
Wrexham General
Wrexham Central
Watery Road Goods & Williams

1) Ellesmere Port Cawoods Coal Terminal
2) Prescot – BICC
3) MSC Loco Depot
4) Chester C & W Shops
5) Manisty Wharf
6) Hayes Chemicals
7) Ellesmere Port Yard and Loco H.S.
8) Tarmac Stone Term.
9) Tanhouse lane – Blue Circle Cement & Plasmor Brick Terminals
10) United Glass Works (Disused)
11) Pilkington's Oil Terminal
12) ICI Works
13) Railcar Services
14) Associated Octel

Wrenbury

Acton Grange Junc.
Berwyn
Berwyn Loop
Berwyn Tun.
Llangollen
Deeside
LLANGOLLEN RAILWAY
Ruabon

CLWYD

Whitchurch

Chirk – Kronospan Wks.
Chirk

Coal Depot -Smallshaw
Gobowen
Gobowen South Junc.
Whittington (Proposed)
Whittington – BP

a) Hartford C.L.C. Junc.
b) Hartford L.N.W. Junc.
c) Parkside W. Junc.
d) Chester North Junc.
e) Parkside Junc.
f) Croes Newydd North Fork
g) West Cheshire Junc.
h) Huyton Junc.
j) Chester South Junc.

k) Lowton Junc.
l) Carterhouse Junc.

Prees

Wem

SHROPSHIRE

Blodwell–ARC (Disused)

Yorton

51

1   40   2

0   5   10 m.
(1:350,000)
0   5   10   15 km.

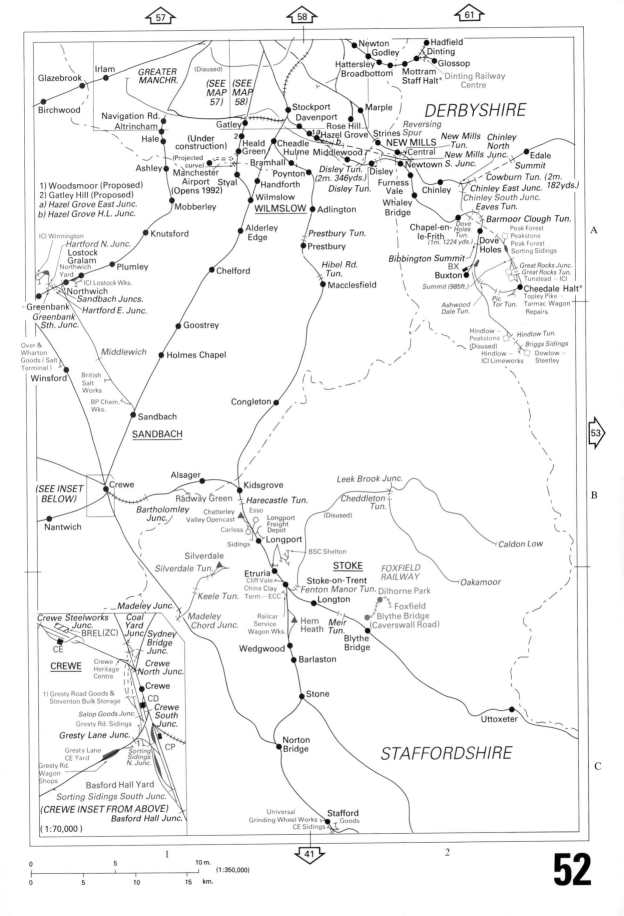

Glazebrook
Irlam
Birchwood

GREATER MANCHR.

(Disused)

(SEE MAP 57) (SEE MAP 58)

Navigation Rd.
Altrincham
Hale
Ashley

(Under construction)

Heald Green

(Projected curve)

Manchester Airport Styal
(Opens 1992)

Mobberley

Knutsford

ICI Winnington
Hartford N. Junc.
Lostock Gralam
Northwich Yard
ICI Lostock Wks.
Northwich
Sandbach Juncs.
Hartford E. Junc.

Greenbank
Greenbank Sth. Junc.

Over & Wharton Goods (Salt Terminal)
Winsford

Middlewich

British Salt Works
BP Chem. Wks.
Sandbach

SANDBACH

Plumley

Chelford

Goostrey

Holmes Chapel

Newton
Godley
Hadfield
Dinting
Hattersley
Broadbottom
Glossop
Mottram Staff Halt*
Dinting Railway Centre

DERBYSHIRE

Stockport
Davenport
Marple
Rose Hill

Gatley

Cheadle
Hulme Middlewood
Bramhall
Poynton
Handforth
Wilmslow

Hazel Grove
a b
Strines
Reversing Spur
New Mills Tun.
NEW MILLS
Central
New Mills S. Junc.
Newtown
Disley
Furness Vale
Whaley Bridge
Chinley North Junc.
Edale
Summit
Cowburn Tun. (2m. 182yds.)
Chinley East Junc.
Chinley South Junc.
Eaves Tun.

Reversing Spur

Disley Tun. (2m. 346yds.)
Disley Tun.

WILMSLOW

Alderley Edge

Adlington

Prestbury Tun.
Prestbury

Hibel Rd. Tun.
Macclesfield

1) Woodsmoor (Proposed)
2) Gatley Hill (Proposed)
a) Hazel Grove East Junc.
b) Hazel Grove H.L. Junc.

Chapel-en-le-Frith
Dove Holes Tun. (1m. 1224yds.)
Dove Holes

Barmoor Clough Tun.
Peak Forest
Peakstone
Peak Forest Sorting Sidings

Bibbington Summit
BX
Buxton
Summit (985ft.)

Great Rocks Junc.
Great Rocks Tun.
Tunstead – ICI

Cheedale Halt*

Topley Pike – Tarmac Wagon Repairs

Ashwood Dale Tun.
Pic Tor Tun.

Hindlow – Peakstone (Disused)
Hindlow – ICI Limeworks

Hindlow Tun.
Briggs Sidings
Dowlow – Steetley

Alsager
Kidsgrove
Radway Green
Harecastle Tun.
Bartholomley Junc.

Chatterley Valley Opencast
Esso
Carless
Sidings

Longport Freight Depot
Longport

BSC Shelton

Leek Brook Junc.

Cheddleton Tun.
(Disused)

Caldon Low

STOKE

FOXFIELD RAILWAY

Oakamoor

Crewe

(SEE INSET BELOW)

Nantwich

Silverdale
Silverdale Tun.

Madeley Junc.

Keele Tun.

Etruria
Cliff Vale
China Clay Term.– ECC

Stoke-on-Trent
Fenton Manor Tun.
Longton

Dilhorne Park
Foxfield
Blythe Bridge (Caverswall Road)

Madeley Chord Junc.

Railcar Service Wagon Wks.

Hem Heath

Meir Tun.
Blythe Bridge

Wedgwood

Barlaston

Uttoxeter

Stone

STAFFORDSHIRE

Crewe Steelworks Junc.
BREL (ZC)
CE

Coal Yard Junc.
Sydney Bridge Junc.

Crewe Heritage Centre
Crewe North Junc.

CREWE

1) Gresty Road Goods & Steventon Bulk Storage

Salop Goods Junc.
Gresty Rd. Sidings
Gresty Lane Junc.

Gresty Lane CE Yard
Gresty Rd. Wagon Shops

Crewe
CD
Crewe South Junc.
CP

Sorting Sidings N. Junc.

Basford Hall Yard
Sorting Sidings South Junc.

(CREWE INSET FROM ABOVE)
Basford Hall Junc.

(1:70,000)

Norton Bridge

Universal Grinding Wheel Works
CE Sidings
Stafford
Goods

A

B

C

1   2

0   5   10 m.   (1:350,000)
0   5   10   15 km.

52

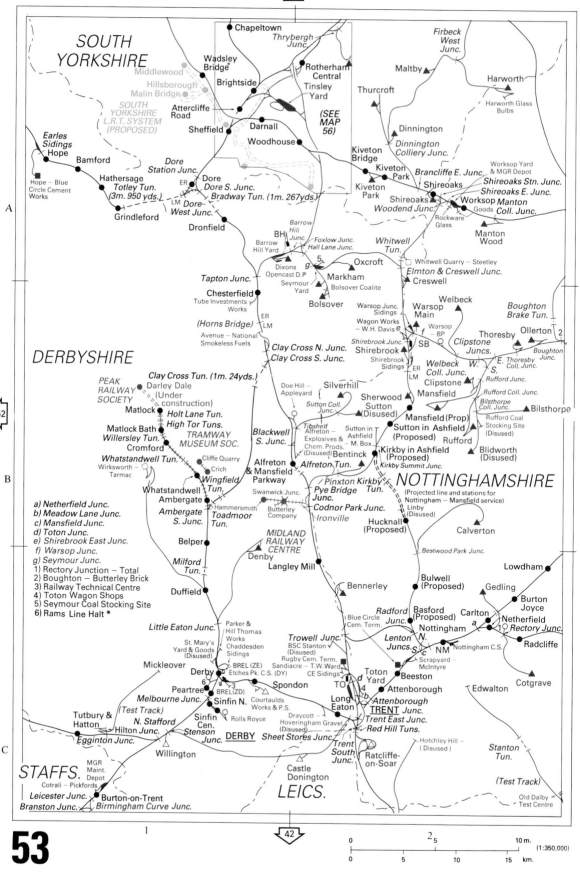

SOUTH
YORKSHIRE

Chapeltown
Thrybergh Junc.

Wadsley
Bridge
Middlewood
Hillsborough
Malin Bridge
SOUTH YORKSHIRE L.R.T. SYSTEM (PROPOSED)

Brightside

Rotherham
Central
Tinsley
Yard

Attercliffe
Road

Sheffield
Darnall
Woodhouse

(SEE MAP 56)

Maltby ▲

Harworth ▲

Thurcroft ▲

Harworth Glass
Bulbs

Firbeck
West
Junc.

Dinnington

*Dinnington
Colliery Junc.*

Worksop Yard
& MGR Depot

*Earles
Sidings*
Hope
Bamford

*Dore
Station Junc.*

Dore
ER *Dore S. Junc.*
Bradway Tun. (1m. 267yds.)
LM *Dore
West Junc.*

Hathersage
*Totley Tun.
(3m. 950 yds.)*

Hope – Blue
Circle Cement
Works

Grindleford

Dronfield

Kiveton
Bridge
Kiveton
Park
Kiveton
Park

Brancliffe E. Junc.
Shireoaks
Shireoaks Stn. Junc.
Shireoaks E. Junc.
Worksop Manton
Coll. Junc.

Shireoaks
Woodend Junc.

Rockware
Glass

Manton
Goods

Manton
Wood ▲

A

Tapton Junc.

BH
*Barrow
Hill
Junc.*
Barrow
Hill Yard

Foxlow Junc.
Hall Lane Junc.

Dixons
Opencast D.P
g
Seymour
Yard

Markham
Bolsover Coalite

Oxcroft ▲

*Whitwell
Tun.*

Whitwell Quarry – Steetley

Elmton & Creswell Junc.
Creswell

Welbeck ▲

*Boughton
Brake Tun.*

Chesterfield
Tube Investments
Works

(Horns Bridge)
ER
LM

Avenue – National
Smokeless Fuels

Bolsover ▲

DERBYSHIRE

Warsop Junc.
Sidings

Wagon Works
– W.H. Davis *e*

*Warsop
Main* ▲
f Warsop
– BP
SB

Thoresby ▲

Ollerton
2

Clay Cross N. Junc.
Clay Cross S. Junc.

Shirebrook Junc.
Shirebrook ▲

Shirebrook
Sidings
ER
LM

*Clipstone
Juncs.*

E. Thoresby
Coll. Junc.

*Boughton
Junc.*

*Welbeck W.
Coll. Junc. S.*

Rufford Junc.

Clay Cross Tun. (1m. 24yds.)

Peak
Railway
Society
Darley Dale
(Under
construction)

Matlock

Holt Lane Tun.
High Tor Tuns.

Doe Hill –
Appleyard

Silverhill ▲

Clipstone

Rufford Coll. Junc.

Mansfield

Bilsthorpe
Coll. Junc.

Bilsthorpe ▲

52

Matlock Bath
Willersley Tun.
Cromford

Whatstandwell Tun.

*TRAMWAY
MUSEUM SOC.*

Wirksworth –
Tarmac

Cliffe Quarry
Crich

*Blackwell
S. Junc.*

Sutton Coll.
Junc.

Tibshelf –
Alfreton –
Explosives &
Chem. Prods.
(Disused)

Sherwood
Sutton
(Disused)

Sutton in
Ashfield –
M. Box

Mansfield (Prop)
*Sutton in Ashfield
(Proposed)*

Rufford Coal
Stocking Site
(Disused)

Rufford ▲

Blidworth
(Disused)

B

a) Netherfield Junc.
b) Meadow Lane Junc.
c) Mansfield Junc.
d) Toton Junc.
e) Shirebrook East Junc.
f) Warsop Junc.
g) Seymour Junc.
1) Rectory Junction – Total
2) Boughton – Butterley Brick
3) Railway Technical Centre
4) Toton Wagon Shops
5) Seymour Coal Stocking Site
6) Rams Line Halt *

*Wingfield
Tun.*
Whatstandwell
Ambergate
*Ambergate
S. Junc.*

Hammersmith
*Toadmoor
Tun.*
Swanwick Junc.
Butterley
Company

Bentinck ▲
Alfreton
& Mansfield
Parkway
Alfreton Tun.

Kirkby Summit Junc.

Kirkby in
Ashfield
(Proposed)

NOTTINGHAMSHIRE

*Pinxton Kirkby
Pye Bridge Tun.*
Junc.
Codnor Park Junc.
Ironville

*(Projected line and stations for
Nottingham – Mansfield service)*
Linby
(Disused)

Belper

*MIDLAND
RAILWAY
CENTRE*
Denby

Langley Mill

Hucknall
(Proposed)

Bestwood Park Junc.

Calverton ▲

*Milford
Tun.*

Bennerley ▲

Bulwell
(Proposed)

Lowdham

Duffield

Radford
Junc.
Basford
(Proposed)

Gedling ▲

Burton
Joyce

Little Eaton Junc.

Parker &
Hill Thomas
Works
Chaddesden
Sidings

St. Mary's
Yard & Goods
(Disused)

Trowell Junc.
BSC Stanton
(Disused)
Rugby Cem. Term.
Sandiacre – T.W. Ward
CE Sidings

Blue Circle
Cem. Term.

*Lenton
Juncs. S.*
N.
NM
Nottingham C.S.

Carlton
a
Netherfield
Rectory Junc.

Radcliffe ▲

Mickleover

Derby
BREL (ZE)
Etches Pk. C.S. (DY)

Scrapyard –
McIntyre

Nottingham

(Test Track)
6
Peartree
3
Melbourne Junc.
Sinfin N.
BREL (ZD)

Spondon

Courtaulds
Works & P.S.

*Toton
TO Yard
4
d b*

*Trent
Junc.*
Beeston

Attenborough

Edwalton

Cotgrave ▲

Tutbury &
Hatton

N. Stafford
Hilton Junc.
Sinfin
Cen.
Stenson
Junc.

Rolls Royce

DERBY
Sheet Stores Junc.

Draycott –
Hoveringham Gravel
(Disused)

Long
Eaton
Attenborough

*TRENT
Trent East Junc.
Red Hill Tuns.*

*Stanton
Tun.*

Egginton Junc.

Willington

Castle
Donington

*Trent
South
Junc.*
Ratcliffe-
on-Soar

Hotchley Hill –
(Disused)

(Test Track)

C

STAFFS.

MGR
Maint.
Depot
Cotrali – Pickfords

Leicester Junc.
Branston Junc.

Burton-on-Trent
Birmingham Curve Junc.

LEICS.

Old Dalby
Test Centre

53

0   5   10 m.
0   5   10   15   km.
(1:350,000)

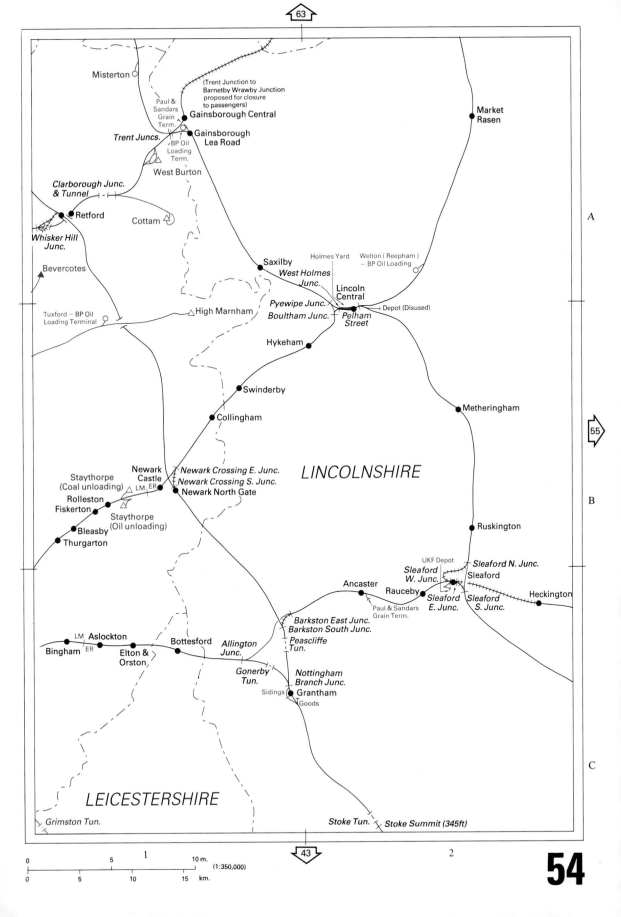

Misterton

(Trent Junction to
Barnetby Wrawby Junction
proposed for closure
to passengers)

Paul &
Sandars
Grain
Term.
Gainsborough Central

Trent Juncs.
**Gainsborough
Lea Road**
BP Oil
Loading
Term.

West Burton

Market
Rasen

*Clarborough Junc.
& Tunnel*

Retford
Cottam

*Whisker Hill
Junc.*

Holmes Yard
Welton (Reepham)
– BP Oil Loading

Saxilby
*West Holmes
Junc.*

Bevercotes

Lincoln
Central

Tuxford – BP Oil
Loading Terminal
High Marnham
Pyewipe Junc.
Boultham Junc.
**Pelham
Street**
Depot (Disused)

Hykeham

LINCOLNSHIRE

Swinderby

Collingham

Metheringham

Newark
Castle
Newark Crossing E. Junc.
Newark Crossing S. Junc.
Newark North Gate

Staythorpe
(Coal unloading)
LM | ER

Rolleston
Fiskerton
Staythorpe
(Oil unloading)

Ruskington

Bleasby
Thurgarton

UKF Depot
Sleaford N. Junc.
*Sleaford
W. Junc.*
Sleaford

Ancaster
Rauceby
*Sleaford
E. Junc.*
*Sleaford
S. Junc.*
Heckington

Paul & Sandars
Grain Term.

LM | Aslockton
Bingham | ER
Elton &
Orston
Bottesford
*Allington
Junc.*

Barkston East Junc.
Barkston South Junc.
*Peascliffe
Tun.*

*Gonerby
Tun.*

*Nottingham
Branch Junc.*
Sidings | **Grantham**
Goods

LEICESTERSHIRE

Grimston Tun.

Stoke Tun. | *Stoke Summit (345ft)*

A

55

B

C

0   1   10 m.
5   (1:350,000)

0   5   10   15   km.

54

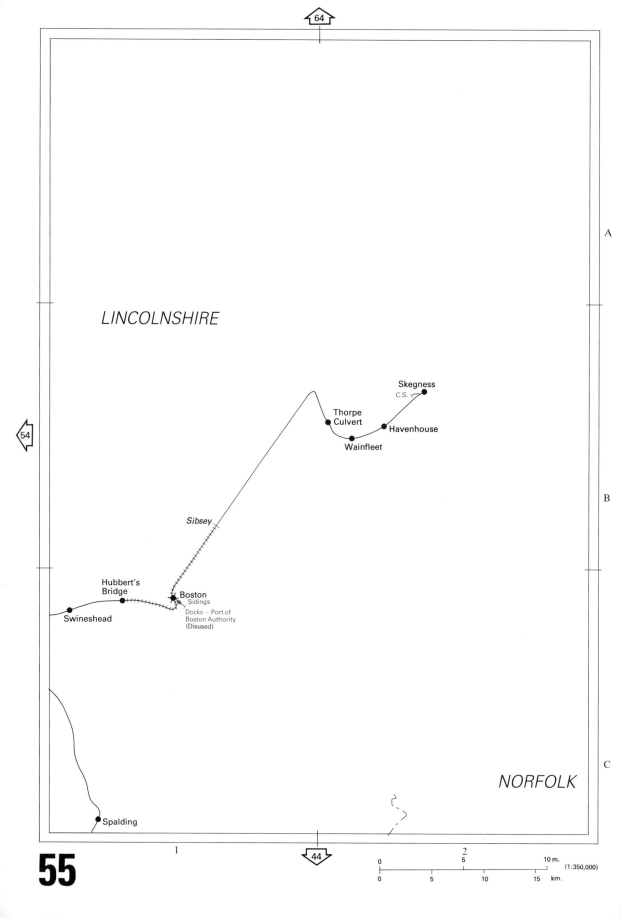

64

A

LINCOLNSHIRE

54

Skegness
C.S.

Thorpe
Culvert

Havenhouse

Wainfleet

B

Sibsey

Hubbert's
Bridge

Boston
Sidings

Docks – Port of
Boston Authority
(Disused)

Swineshead

C

NORFOLK

Spalding

1

44

2
5

0   10 m.
                                    (1:350,000)

0   5   10   15   km.

55

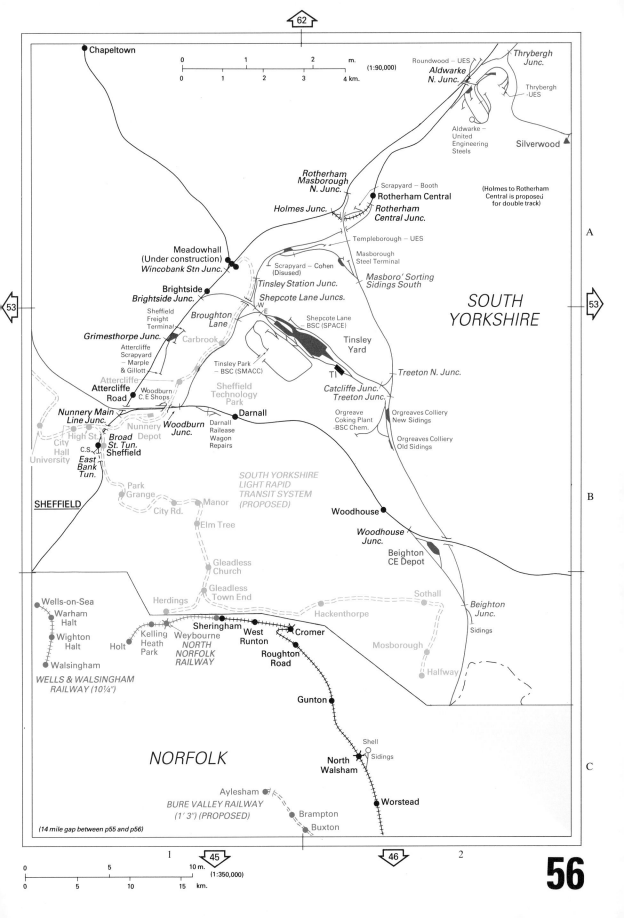

● Chapeltown

0   1   2   m.   (1:90,000)

0   1   2   3   4 km.

Roundwood – UES
Thrybergh Junc.
Aldwarke N. Junc.
Thrybergh – UES
Aldwarke – United Engineering Steels
Silverwood ▲

Rotherham Masborough N. Junc.
Scrapyard – Booth
● Rotherham Central
Rotherham Central Junc.
Holmes Junc.
(Holmes to Rotherham Central is proposed for double track)

Templeborough – UES

Meadowhall (Under construction)
Wincobank Stn Junc.
Scrapyard – Cohen (Disused)
Masborough Steel Terminal
Masboro' Sorting Sidings South

Brightside
Brightside Junc.
Tinsley Station Junc.
Shepcote Lane Juncs.
W
E

SOUTH YORKSHIRE

Broughton Lane
Shepcote Lane BSC (SPACE)
Sheffield Freight Terminal
Grimesthorpe Junc.
Carbrook
Attercliffe Scrapyard – Marple & Gillott
Tinsley Park – BSC (SMACC)
Tinsley Yard
TI

Attercliffe
Attercliffe Road
Woodburn C.E Shops
Sheffield Technology Park
Catcliffe Junc.
Treeton Junc.
Treeton N. Junc.

Nunnery Main Line Junc.
Nunnery Depot
Woodburn Junc.
● Darnall
Darnall Railease Wagon Repairs
Orgreave Coking Plant -BSC Chem.
Orgreaves Colliery New Sidings
Orgreaves Colliery Old Sidings

High St.
Broad St. Tun.
● Sheffield
C.S.
East Bank Tun.
City Hall University

SHEFFIELD

Park Grange
City Rd.
● Manor
● Elm Tree

SOUTH YORKSHIRE LIGHT RAPID TRANSIT SYSTEM (PROPOSED)

● Woodhouse
Woodhouse Junc.
Beighton CE Depot

Gleadless Church
Gleadless Town End
Sothall
Beighton Junc.
Sidings

● Wells-on-Sea
Warham Halt
Wighton Halt
● Walsingham
Holt
Kelling Heath Park
Herdings
Sheringham
Weybourne
NORTH NORFOLK RAILWAY
West Runton
★ Cromer
Roughton Road
Hackenthorpe
Mosborough
Halfway

WELLS & WALSINGHAM RAILWAY (10¼")

● Gunton

NORFOLK

Shell Sidings
North Walsham ★

A

B

C

Aylesham
BURE VALLEY RAILWAY (1' 3") (PROPOSED)
Brampton
Buxton
Worstead ●

(14 mile gap between p55 and p56)

0   5   10 m.
(1:350,000)
0   5   10   15 km.

1   2

53

56

Moses Gate

Farnworth

Farnworth Tuns.

Kearsley

Walkden

Moorside

Swinton

Pendlebury Tun.

Clifton

Whitefield

Whitefield Tun.

Besses-o'-th'-Barn

Prestwich

Heaton Park

Heaton Park Tun.

Bowker Vale

A

Stone Terminal – Tarmac

Brindle Heath – Greater Manchester Waste Disposal Agency

Windsor Bridge Junc.

Pendleton

Salford Crescent

Deal St. Junc.

Salford

Patricroft

Eccles

Weaste – Lancs. Tar Distillers

Hope Street Stone Term. Peakstone

Liverpool Road

G-MEX Central

2

Cerestar Works

Langworthy

Ordsall La Junc.

Trafford Park Industrial Estate

Norton Metals Scrapyard

Broadway (Salford Quays)

Dock 9

Pomona

Deansgate

Trafford Park

Dock 7

Ordsall

Castlefield Junc.

Trafford Park Estate – MSC Loco Shed

Cornbrook Junc.

Containerbase

GEC Wks. (Disused)

FLT MIFT

Old Trafford Tun.

B

Higher Irlam

Davyhulme

Barton Dock MSC Loco Shed

1 a

Trafford Park Sidings

Old Trafford

Throstle Nest Tuns.

Warwick Rd. for Old Trafford

Trafford Park

Humphrey Park

Urmston

Chassen Road

Stretford

Manchester Road

(Disused)

52

Flixton

Chorlton-cum-Hardy

St. Werburgh's Road

Glazebrook East Junc.

Irlam

Glazebrook – British Tar Products

Dane Road

Cadishead

Partington

Partington Shell Oil Ref. & Chem. Wks.

Sale

a) Trafford Park E. Junc.

1) Manchester United Football Ground*

2) Ordsall Lane-Faber-Prest (Otis Euro)

Brooklands

(Deansgate Junc. to Altrincham to be parallel Metrolink and BR lines)

C

Timperley

Deansgate Junc.

Skelton Junc.

Navigation Road

Northenden Blue Circle Cement Term.

57

1

2

0   1   2   m.

0   1   2   3   4 km.

(1:90,000)

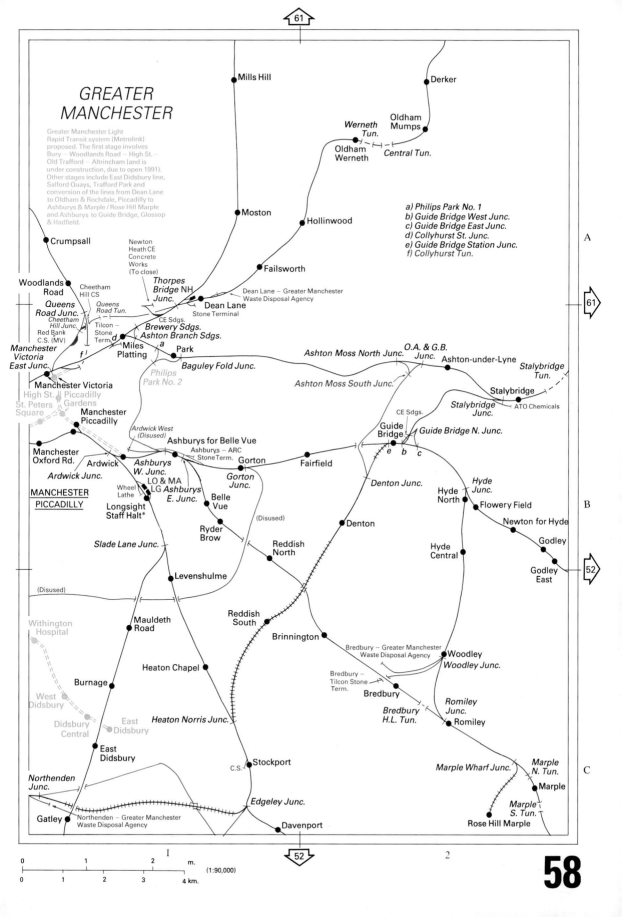

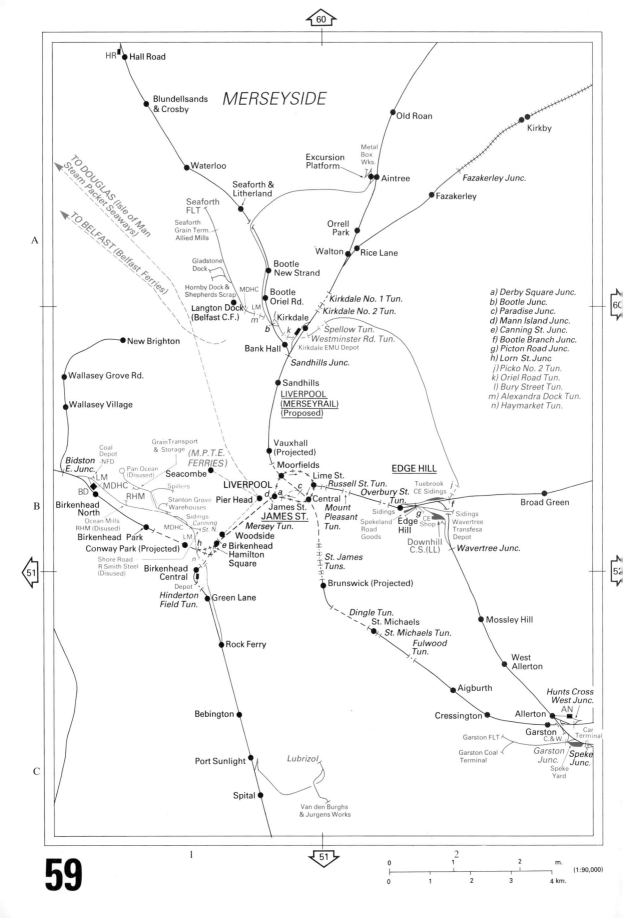

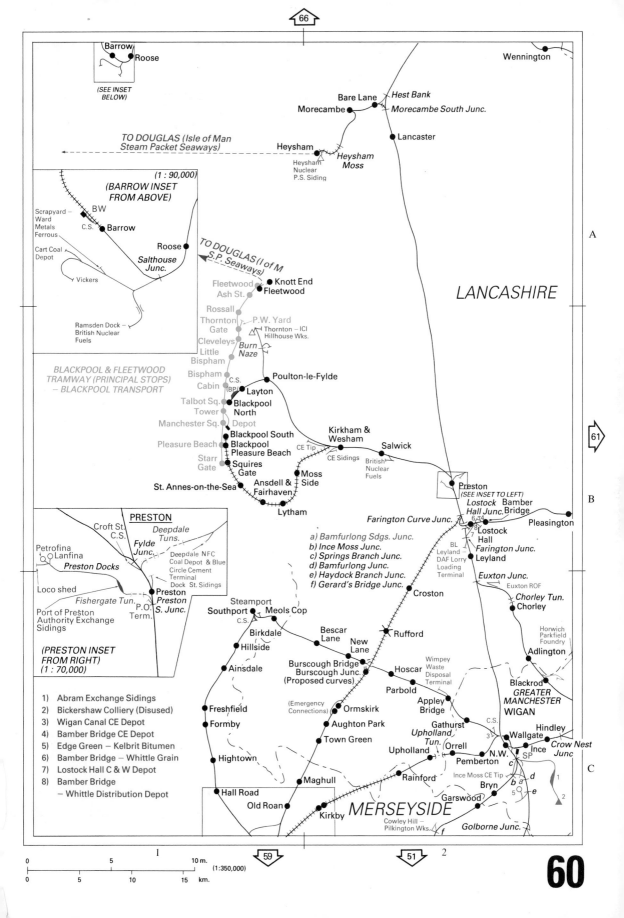

Barrow
Roose

(SEE INSET BELOW)

Wennington

Bare Lane   *Hest Bank*
Morecambe   *Morecambe South Junc.*

Lancaster

TO DOUGLAS (Isle of Man Steam Packet Seaways)

Heysham   *Heysham Moss*

Heysham Nuclear P.S. Siding

(1 : 90,000)
(BARROW INSET FROM ABOVE)

Scrapyard – Ward Metals Ferrous
BW
C.S.   Barrow

Cart Coal Depot

Vickers

Roose
Salthouse Junc.

TO DOUGLAS (I of M S.P. Seaways)

Ramsden Dock – British Nuclear Fuels

LANCASHIRE

Knott End
Fleetwood   Ash St.   Fleetwood

Rossall
Thornton Gate
Cleveleys
Little Bispham   *Burn Naze*

P.W. Yard
Thornton – ICI Hillhouse Wks.

BLACKPOOL & FLEETWOOD TRAMWAY (PRINCIPAL STOPS) – BLACKPOOL TRANSPORT

Bispham
Cabin   C.S.   (BP)

Talbot Sq.   Layton
Tower   **Blackpool North**
Manchester Sq.   Depot

Poulton-le-Fylde

Pleasure Beach

Starr Gate

Blackpool South
Blackpool Pleasure Beach
Squires Gate

St. Annes-on-the-Sea

Ansdell & Fairhaven

Lytham

Kirkham & Wesham

Salwick

CE Tip
CE Sidings
British Nuclear Fuels

Moss Side

Preston
(SEE INSET TO LEFT)

Lostock Hall Junc.   Bamber Bridge

Faringtan Curve Junc.

Lostock Hall
Farington Junc.
BL Leyland – DAF Lorry Loading Terminal   Leyland

Pleasington

a) Bamfurlong Sdgs. Junc.
b) Ince Moss Junc.
c) Springs Branch Junc.
d) Bamfurlong Junc.
e) Haydock Branch Junc.
f) Gerard's Bridge Junc.

Euxton Junc.
Euxton ROF   *Chorley Tun.*
Chorley

PRESTON
Croft St.   C.S.
Deepdale Tuns.
Fylde Junc.
Deepdale NFC Coal Depot & Blue Circle Cement Terminal
Dock St. Sidings
Petrofina
Lanfina
Preston Docks
Loco shed
Fishergate Tun.
Port of Preston Authority Exchange Sidings
P.O. Term.   Preston   Preston S. Junc.

(PRESTON INSET FROM RIGHT) (1 : 70,000)

Croston

Steamport
Southport   Meols Cop
C.S.

Rufford

Horwich Parkfield Foundry

Adlington

1) Abram Exchange Sidings
2) Bickershaw Colliery (Disused)
3) Wigan Canal CE Depot
4) Bamber Bridge CE Depot
5) Edge Green – Kelbrit Bitumen
6) Bamber Bridge – Whittle Grain
7) Lostock Hall C & W Depot
8) Bamber Bridge – Whittle Distribution Depot

Birkdale
Hillside
Ainsdale

Bescar Lane
New Lane

Burscough Bridge
Burscough Junc. (Proposed curves)

Hoscar

Wimpey Waste Disposal Terminal

Parbold

Appley Bridge

GREATER MANCHESTER
Blackrod
WIGAN

Freshfield
Formby

(Emergency Connections)

Ormskirk

Aughton Park
Town Green

Gathurst
C.S.
Upholland Tun.
Orrell
Upholland
Pemberton

Hindley
Wallgate
Ince
Crow Nest Junc.
N.W.   SP

Hightown

Rainford

Ince Moss CE Tip

Bryn
Garswood

Maghull

Hall Road
Old Roan   Kirkby

MERSEYSIDE

Cowley Hill – Pilkington Wks.

Golborne Junc.

0   5   10 m.
(1:350,000)
0   5   10   15   km.

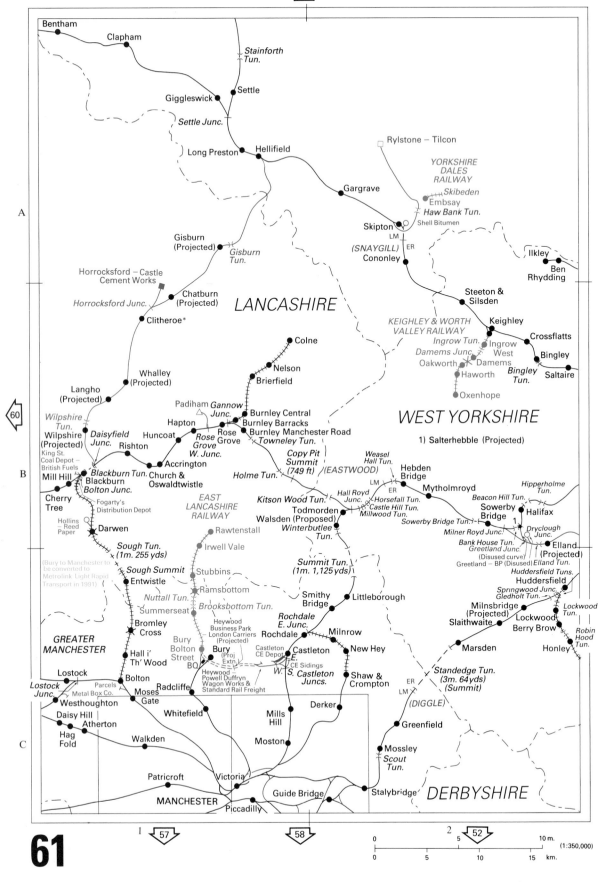

Bentham

Clapham

Stainforth Tun.

Settle

Giggleswick

Settle Junc.

Long Preston Hellifield

Gargrave

Rylstone – Tilcon

YORKSHIRE DALES RAILWAY

Skibeden

Embsay

Haw Bank Tun.

Shell Bitumen

Skipton

LM

(SNAYGILL) ER

Cononley

Ilkley

Ben Rhydding

A

Gisburn (Projected)

Gisburn Tun.

Horrocksford – Castle Cement Works

Horrocksford Junc.

Chatburn (Projected)

Clitheroe*

LANCASHIRE

Steeton & Silsden

Keighley

KEIGHLEY & WORTH VALLEY RAILWAY

Ingrow Tun.

Ingrow West

Crossflatts

Bingley

Damems Junc.

Damems

Oakworth

Bingley Tun.

Saltaire

Whalley (Projected)

Colne

Nelson

Brierfield

Haworth

Oxenhope

WEST YORKSHIRE

Langho (Projected)

Wilpshire Tun.

Wilpshire (Projected)

Padiham *Gannow Junc.*

Hapton

Huncoat

Daisyfield Junc.

Rishton

Rose Grove W. Junc.

Rose Grove

Burnley Central

Burnley Barracks

Burnley Manchester Road

Towneley Tun.

1) Salterhebble (Projected)

King St. Coal Depot – British Fuels

B

Blackburn Tun.

Blackburn

Blackburn Bolton Junc.

Mill Hill

Cherry Tree

Accrington

Church & Oswaldtwistle

Copy Pit Summit (749 ft)

(EASTWOOD)

Holme Tun.

Weasel Hall Tun.

Hebden Bridge

LM

ER

Mytholmroyd

Hipperholme Tun.

Fogarty's Distribution Depot

EAST LANCASHIRE RAILWAY

Kitson Wood Tun.

Hall Royd Junc.

Castle Hill Tun.

Beacon Hill Tun.

Sowerby Bridge

Halifax

Hollins – Reed Paper

Darwen

Todmorden

Walsden (Proposed)

Millwood Tun.

Sowerby Bridge Tun.

Milner Royd Junc.

1

Dryclough Junc.

Sough Tun. (1m. 255 yds)

Winterbutlee Tun.

Bank House Tun.

Greetland Junc.

(Disused curve)

Elland (Projected)

Greetland – BP (Disused) *Elland Tun.*

(Bury to Manchester to be converted to Metrolink Light Rapid Transport in 1991)

Sough Summit

Entwistle

Nuttall Tun.

Summerseat

Brooksbottom Tun.

Rawtenstall

Irwell Vale

Stubbins

Ramsbottom

Summit Tun. (1m. 1,125 yds)

Smithy Bridge

Littleborough

Huddersfield Tuns.

Huddersfield

Springwood Junc.

Gledholt Tun.

Bromley Cross

Hall i' Th' Wood

Heywood Business Park – London Carriers (Projected)

Rochdale E. Junc.

Rochdale

Milnrow

Milnsbridge (Projected)

Slaithwaite

Lockwood

Lockwood Tun.

Robin Hood Tun.

GREATER MANCHESTER

Lostock

Lostock Junc.

Bolton

Radcliffe

Bury Bolton Street

BQ.

Castleton CE Depot

E.

W.

Castleton

S. Castleton Juncs.

New Hey

Shaw & Crompton

Berry Brow

Honley

Parcels

Metal Box Co.

Heywood Powell Duffryn Wagon Works & Standard Rail Freight

CE Sidings

Marsden

Standedge Tun. (3m. 64 yds) (Summit)

ER

LM

(DIGGLE)

C

Daisy Hill

Hag Fold

Atherton

Westhoughton

Moses Gate

Whitefield

Derker

Greenfield

Walkden

Mills Hill

Moston

Mossley

Scout Tun.

Patricroft

Victoria

Guide Bridge

Stalybridge

DERBYSHIRE

MANCHESTER

Piccadilly

YORK

(YORK INSET FROM RIGHT)

NORTH YORKSHIRE

Poppleton

Skelton Junc.

British Sugar Wks.

York Yard North Sidings
York Yard North

Leeman Road CE Depot & CE Works   YK

National Railway Museum

National Railway Museum Annexe

Up Yard

BREL Carriage Works (ZR)
York Yard South

York

S & T Service Centre
Wagon Repair Shops

Holgate Junc.
Holgate Sidings

(1:90,000)

1) Pontefract Tanshelf (Projected)
2) Featherstone (Projected)
3) Streethouse (Projected)

Knaresborough Tun.

4) Dewsbury – Blue Circle Cem. Term.
5) Wakefield Kirkgate S & T Sidings
6) Laisterdyke – Bamforth Scrapyard
7) Cobra Freight Terminal
8) Scrapyard – Crossley Evans
9) Knottingley – Rockware Glass
a) Calder Bridge Junc.
b) Oakenshaw Junc.
c) Oakenshaw South Junc.
d) Knottingley South Junc.
e) Crofton West Junc.

f) Knottingley East Junc.
g) Knottingley West Junc.
h) Horbury Junc.

j) Ferrybridge Junc.
k) Turners Lane Junc.
l) Kirkgate West Junc.
m) Westgate South Junc.
n) Pontefract Monkhill Goods Junc.
p) Pontefract West Junc.
q) Dewsbury East Junc.
r) Horbury Station Junc.
s) Thornhill L.N.W. Junc.
t) Shipley Bingley Junc.
u) Shipley Bradford Junc.
v) Shipley Guiseley Junc.

A

Starbeck
Shell
Harrogate
Knaresborough   Hammerton   Cattal
Hessay

YORK
Poppleton   York   *(SEE INSET TO LEFT)*

Pannal

Weeton

Wescoehill Tun.

WEST YORKSHIRE

Colton Junc.

Burley-in-Wharfedale
Menston

Greenbottom Tun. Guiseley
Baildon Tuns.
Baildon   *Esholt Tun.*
Thackley Tun.
Apperley Junc.
Shipley
Frizinghall
New Bradford Pudsey Forster Sq.

Bramhope Tun. (2m 241yds)

Horsforth
Hawksworth (Projected)
(SEE INSET P.63)
Headingley

Ulleskelf
Church Fenton

Sherburn South Junc.
Sherburn in Elmet

Selby N. Side Discharge Sdg.
Selby Swing Bridge & Freight
Selby Storage

LEEDS
Leeds

Cross Gates   East Garforth   Garforth   South Milford   Selby Drift Mine
Micklefield   Milford Junc.

Selby West Junc.   Selby
E. Selby Goods Viking Shipping

Bramley
Stanningley Tun.
Armley (Projected)
Cottingley

Mill Lane Junc.
Bradford Interchange
Wakefield Rd. Tun.
Bowling Tun.

B

Morley

Woodlesford

Bowers Row (Disused)
Castleford East Junc.
Allerton Bywater

Milford Sidings
Gascoigne Wood Junc.
W. Hambleton Juncs.
(Proposed Curves)

Brayton Junc.
Barlow Branch (CE Test Track)

Selby Canal Junc.
Drax
Sdgs

Wyke Tun.
Brighouse (Projected)

Morley Tun. (1m 1609 yds.)
Ardsley Tun.
Batley
Outwood

Methley Junc.
Castleford W. Junc.
(Altofts is proposed for closure)

Altofts
Altofts Junc.
Castleford
Whitwood Junc.

Ferrybridge
Brotherton Tun.
Knottingley
Kellingley
Sudforth Lane

Temple Hirst Junc.
Whitley Bridge   Hensall   Snaith
Hensall Junc.
Heck – Plasmor

Eggborough

Bradley Wood Junc.
Ravensthorpe
Mirfield
Bradley Tun.
Bradley Junc.
Deighton (Proposed)
Heaton Lodge Junc.

Dewsbury
Dewsbury Rly. St. Goods (Disused)
Wakefield Kirkgate
Car Term.
Normanton
Prince of Wales
Sharlston

p
n
g   KY
q
9

Pontefract Monkhill
Pontefract Baghill

Thornhill (Proposed)
HM
HEALEY MILLS   Healey Mills Yard
British Oak (Disused)
Crigglestone Junc.
Procor Wagon Wks.
Crofton CE Depot
Crofton East Junc.
Hare Park Junc.

Sandal & Agbrigg
Fitzwilliam

Norton

Askern

Joan Croft Junc.
Hatfield
Stainforth & Hatfield
Thorne Junc.

C

Brockholes
Stocksmoor
Clayton West Junc.
Thurstonland Tun.   Shepley
Cumberworth Tun.
Denby Dale

Penistone
Wellhouse Tun. Dodworth
Oxspring Tun.
Silkstone Common

Woolley Tuns.
Woolley
Darton
Royston
Monk Bretton – Redfern National Glass

Royston Drift
South Kirkby

Barnsley Station Junc.
Cudworth N. Junc.
Barnsley

Grimethorpe
Coalite
Houghton Main

South Kirkby Junc.
South Elmsall

Moorthorpe   Frickley
Adwick Junc.

Thurnscoe
Hickleton
Goldthorpe
Goldthorpe

Shaftholme Junc.

Hexthorpe Junc.
Doncaster

(SEE INSET P.64)

DONCASTER

SOUTH YORKSHIRE

Wombwell
Elsecar

Bolton-on-Dearne
Swinton Junc.
Swinton
Synthetic Chem. Wks.
Conisbrough Tun.
Mexborough   Conisbrough
Mexborough East Junc.
Kilnhurst Loco Wks.- RFS

Finningley*

Stocksbridge – United Engineering Steels Sdgs.
Tankersley Tun.
Deepcar Tun.

0   5   10 m.
0   5   10   15   km.
(1:350,000)

1   2

63

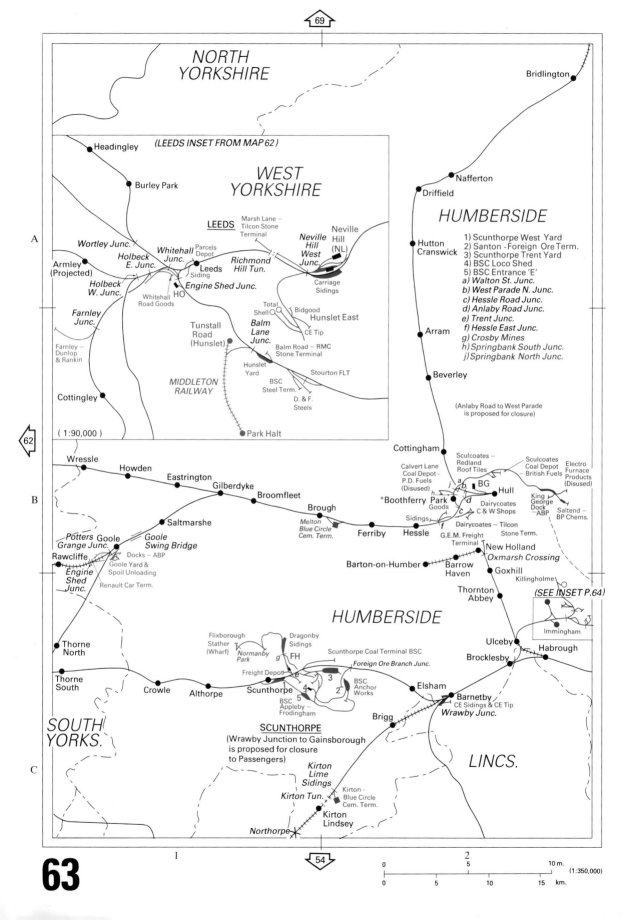

NORTH
YORKSHIRE

Bridlington

(LEEDS INSET FROM MAP 62)

WEST
YORKSHIRE

Headingley

Burley Park

Nafferton

Driffield

HUMBERSIDE

LEEDS

Marsh Lane –
Tilcon Stone
Terminal

Neville
Hill
West
Junc.

Neville
Hill
(NL)

1) Scunthorpe West Yard
2) Santon - Foreign Ore Term.
3) Scunthorpe Trent Yard
4) BSC Loco Shed
5) BSC Entrance 'E'
a) Walton St. Junc.
b) West Parade N. Junc.
c) Hessle Road Junc.
d) Anlaby Road Junc.
e) Trent Junc.
f) Hessle East Junc.
g) Crosby Mines
h) Springbank South Junc.
j) Springbank North Junc.

A

Wortley Junc.

Holbeck
E. Junc.

Whitehall
Junc.

Parcels
Depot

Richmond
Hill Tun.

Armley
(Projected)

Holbeck
W. Junc.

Leeds
Siding

Engine Shed Junc.

Whitehall
Road Goods

HO

Carriage
Sidings

Hutton
Cranswick

Farnley
Junc.

Total
Shell

Bidgood
Hunslet East

Arram

Farnley –
Dunlop
& Rankin

Tunstall
Road
(Hunslet)

Balm
Lane
Junc.

CE Tip

Balm Road – RMC
Stone Terminal

Beverley

Cottingley

MIDDLETON
RAILWAY

Hunslet
Yard

BSC
Steel Term.

Stourton FLT

(Anlaby Road to West Parade
is proposed for closure)

(1:90,000)

Park Halt

D. & F.
Steels

Cottingham

Sculcoates –
Redland
Roof Tiles

Sculcoates
Coal Depot –
British Fuels

Electro
Furnace
Products
(Disused)

B

Wressle

Howden

Eastrington

Gilberdyke

Broomfleet

Calvert Lane
Coal Depot -
P.D. Fuels
(Disused)

a
b
h

BG

*Boothferry Park

Hull

Brough

Saltmarshe

Melton
Blue Circle
Cem. Term.

Ferriby

Goods

d

c

Sidings

Hessle

f

Dairycoates
C & W Shops

King
George
Dock –
ABP

Saltend –
BP Chems.

Dairycoates – Tilcon
Stone Term.

Potters
Grange Junc.

Goole

Goole
Swing Bridge

G.E.M. Freight
Terminal

New Holland
Oxmarsh Crossing

Rawcliffe

Docks – ABP

Barton-on-Humber

Barrow
Haven

Goxhill

Engine
Shed
Junc.

Goole Yard
& Spoil Unloading

Renault Car Term.

Killingholme

Thornton
Abbey

(SEE INSET P.64)

HUMBERSIDE

Immingham

Thorne
North

Flixborough
Stather
(Wharf)

Dragonby
Sidings

Ulceby

Habrough

Thorne
South

Crowle

Normanby
Park

Althorpe

Freight Depot

g

FH

Scunthorpe

Scunthorpe Coal Terminal BSC

Foreign Ore Branch Junc.

BSC
Anchor Works

Elsham

Brocklesby

SOUTH
YORKS.

1

e

4

5

3

2

BSC Appleby –
Frodingham

Barnetby

CE Sidings & CE Tip

Wrawby Junc.

Brigg

LINCS.

C

SCUNTHORPE
(Wrawby Junction to Gainsborough
is proposed for closure
to Passengers)

Kirton
Lime
Sidings

Kirton Tun.

Kirton –
Blue Circle
Cem. Term.

Northorpe

Kirton
Lindsey

63

0   2   10 m.
0 5   10   15 km.
(1:350,000)

Stainforth & Hatfield
Stainforth Junc.
Joan Croft Junc.
Shaftholme Junc.
Skellow Junc.
Applehurst Junc.
Thorpe Marsh
Adwick Junc.
Carcroft Junc.
Skellow–Amoco
Carcroft (Projected)
Kirk Sandall (Proposed)
Brodsworth
Bentley
N.
W.
S.
Bentley Colliery Juncs.
Kirk Sandall Junc.
N. Castle Hills Juncs.
W. S.
Kirk Sandall -Rockware

A

Bentley (Projected)
Bentley Junc.
Markham Main

DONCASTER
Marshgate CE Sidings
RFS Industries (ZB)
Marshgate Junc.
BRML (DL)
Doncaster
Doncaster West Yard
South Yorkshire Junc.
Hexthorpe Sidings
St. James Junc.
Bridge Junc.
DR
Wood Yard CE Depot
Decoy Up Yard
Decoy North Junc.

SOUTH YORKSHIRE

Electrification Depot
Hexthorpe Junc.
Belmont Yard
Black Carr Junc.
Bessacarr Junc.
Goods
Decoy South Junc.
Flyover East Junc.
Flyover West Junc.
Loversall Carr Junc.

1) Stallingborough
2) Healing
3) Great Coates
4) Grimsby Docks
5) Tioxide Works
6) Ciba – Geigy
7) C. Smaller Ft. Term.

B

St. Catherine's Junc.

Rossington

(DONCASTER INSET FROM MAP 62)

(1:90,000)

Immingham Railfreight Terminals
Courtaulds Works
Pyewipe Road
7
W Marsh Sdgs.
6 5
1
2
3 N.
W. E.
4
Docks ABP
New Clee
C.S.
Cleethorpes
Marsh Juncs.
Grimsby Town
Pasture Street

IMMINGHAM TO EMDEN (Train Ferry) & CUXHAVEN (Elbe – Humber Line)

HULL TO ROTTERDAM (EUROPOORT) & ZEEBRUGGE (North Sea Ferries)

(IMMINGHAM INSET FROM MAP 63)

Lindsey – Petrofina & Total
Loco Shed
Coal Terminal – BSC
Texaco
Immingham West Junc.
Ore Terminal – BSC
Immingham Storage
Mineral Quay
Immingham Docks – ABP
Esso
Immingham Storage
Texaco ABM
Humber – Conoco
Humber Road Junc.
Immingham Yard
Coal Terminal – BC
Firegold Plant – Petrofina
C. & W. Shops
IM
Norsk Hydro Wks.

C

LINCOLNSHIRE

(1:90,000)

HUMBERSIDE

Immingham East Junc.

1

10 m.

2

0   5   10 m.   (1:350,000)
0   5   10   15 km.

64

Lakeland ▲ ● Maryport

Flimby
⊢ Broughton
Moor

Siddick Junc.
Derwent Junc.
Docks ⊣ *Calva Junc.*
Leyland Works ● Workington
BSC Goods
Workington

Harrington

Parton

Whitehaven
Preston St. *Whitehaven Tun.*
Albright &
Wilson Terminal ● Corkickle

⊢ Moor Row (Disused)

★ St. Bees

Nethertown

Braystones

Sellafield
Sellafield – British
Nuclear Fuels

Seascale

Drigg –British *Miteside*
Nuclear Fuels ● Drigg

Ravenglass *Muncaster
Mill*

*Vickers
Gun
Range
Eskmeals ⊢ Sidings*

Bootle

Ramsey

Bellevue Lewaigue

ISLE OF MAN RAILWAYS Dreemskerry
(MANX ELECTRIC RAILWAY)
(3'0" Derby Castle -Ramsey) Ballaglass Ballajora
(3'6" Laxey - Snaefell) Cornaa
Glen Mona
Snaefell Dhoon
(1990 ft)
Bungalow Ballaragh

Depot Minorca
Laxey
Fairy Cottage South
Ballabeg Cape
Garwick Glen
Baldrine

*ISLE
OF MAN* *GROUDLE GLEN* Lhen
RAILWAY (2'0") Coan ● Headland
Depots ● Groudle Glen
Derby Castle
DOUGLAS CORP. HORSE TRAMS Onchan Head
(3'0" Pier - Derby Castle) Douglas

TO BELFAST

Douglas
ISLE OF MAN RAILWAYS Port Soderick Pier *TO HEYSHAM*
(STEAM OPERATED) Santon
(3'0") *TO FLEETWOOD*

Colby Ballabeg
Port Erin ● Ballasalla
Port St. Mary Castletown
TO DUBLIN *TO LIVERPOOL*

(All Ships Isle of Man Steam Packet Seaways)

65

0   5   10 m.
0   5   10   15   km.
(1:350,000)

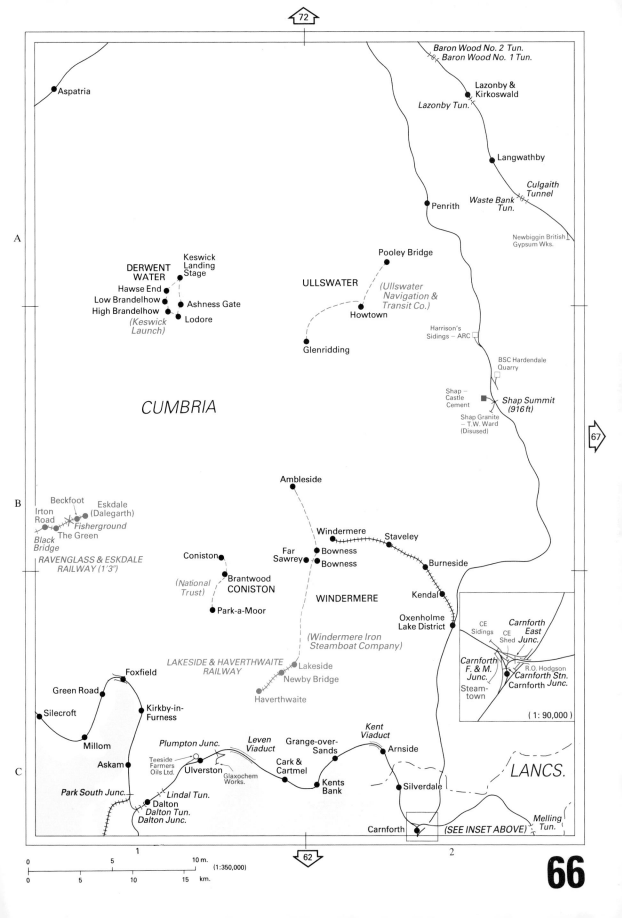

Aspatria

Baron Wood No. 2 Tun.
Baron Wood No. 1 Tun.

Lazonby &
Kirkoswald

Lazonby Tun.

Langwathby

*Culgaith
Tunnel*

Penrith

*Waste Bank
Tun.*

Newbiggin British
Gypsum Wks.

DERWENT
WATER

Keswick
Landing
Stage

Hawse End

Low Brandelhow

High Brandelhow

Ashness Gate

Lodore

*(Keswick
Launch)*

A

Pooley Bridge

ULLSWATER

*(Ullswater
Navigation &
Transit Co.)*

Howtown

Harrison's
Sidings – ARC

Glenridding

BSC Hardendale
Quarry

CUMBRIA

Shap –
Castle Cement

*Shap Summit
(916 ft)*

Shap Granite
– T.W. Ward
(Disused)

Ambleside

B

Beckfoot

Eskdale
(Dalegarth)

Irton
Road

Fisherground

*Black
Bridge*

The Green

*RAVENGLASS & ESKDALE
RAILWAY (1´3˝)*

Coniston

Brantwood
CONISTON

*(National
Trust)*

Park-a-Moor

Windermere

Far
Sawrey

Bowness

Bowness

Staveley

Burneside

Kendal

WINDERMERE

Oxenholme
Lake District

*(Windermere Iron
Steamboat Company)*

CE
Sidings

*Carnforth
East
Junc.*

CE
Shed

*Carnforth
F. & M.
Junc.*

R.O. Hodgson

*LAKESIDE & HAVERTHWAITE
RAILWAY*

Lakeside

Newby Bridge

Haverthwaite

*Carnforth
Stn.
Junc.*

Carnforth

Steam-
town

(1: 90,000)

Foxfield

Green Road

Silecroft

Kirkby-in-
Furness

Millom

Askam

Plumpton Junc.

Teeside
Farmers
Oils Ltd.

Ulverston

Glaxochem
Works.

*Leven
Viaduct*

Grange-over-
Sands

Cark &
Cartmel

*Kent
Viaduct*

Arnside

LANCS.

C

Park South Junc.

Lindal Tun.

Dalton

Dalton Tun.

Dalton Junc.

Kents
Bank

Silverdale

*Melling
Tun.*

Carnforth

(SEE INSET ABOVE)

0   1   5   10 m.
0   5   10   15 km.
(1:350,000)

66

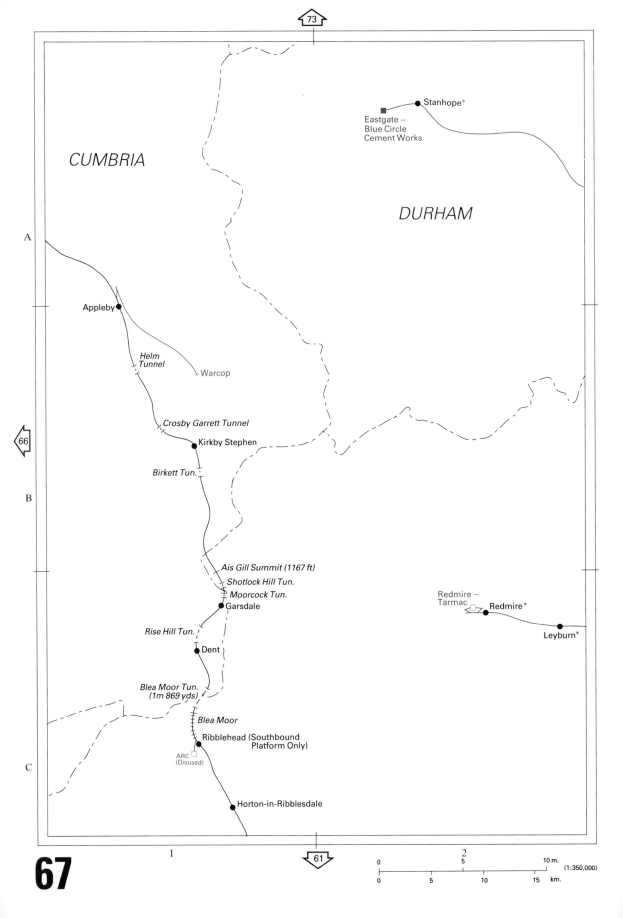

CUMBRIA

DURHAM

Stanhope*

Eastgate –
Blue Circle
Cement Works

A

Appleby

*Helm
Tunnel*

Warcop

Crosby Garrett Tunnel

66

Kirkby Stephen

Birkett Tun.

B

Ais Gill Summit (1167 ft)

Shotlock Hill Tun.

Moorcock Tun.

Garsdale

Redmire –
Tarmac

Redmire*

Rise Hill Tun.

Leyburn*

Dent

Blea Moor Tun.
(1m 869 yds)

Blea Moor

Ribblehead (Southbound
Platform Only)

ARC
(Disused)

C

Horton-in-Ribblesdale

67

0	2	10 m.

0   5   10   15   km.

(1:350,000)

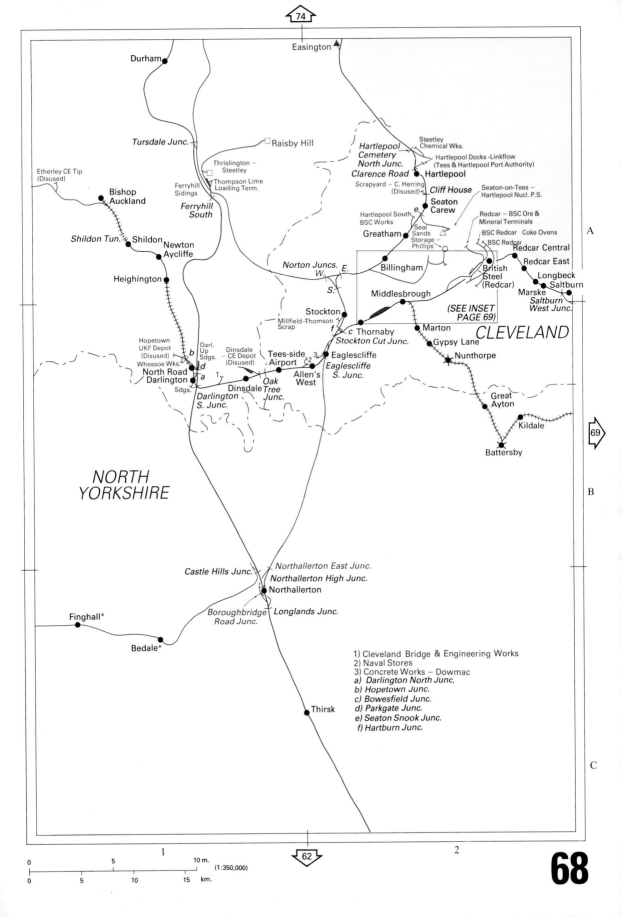

Easington

Durham

Tursdale Junc.

Raisby Hill

Etherley CE Tip (Disused)

Thrislington – Steetley

Hartlepool Cemetery North Junc.
Steetley Chemical Wks.

Ferryhill Sidings
Thompson Lime Loading Term.

Ferryhill South

Clarence Road
Hartlepool Docks -Linkflow (Tees & Hartlepool Port Authority)
Hartlepool

Bishop Auckland

Scrapyard – C. Herring (Disused)
Cliff House
Seaton-on-Tees – Hartlepool Nucl. P.S.

Shildon Tun.
Shildon
Newton Aycliffe

Seaton Carew
e

Hartlepool South BSC Works
Redcar – BSC Ore & Mineral Terminals

Heighington

Greatham
BSC Redcar   Coke Ovens
BSC Redcar
A

Seal Sands Storage – Phillips

Norton Juncs.
W
E.
Billingham
British Steel (Redcar)
Redcar Central

S.
Redcar East

Hopetown UKF Depot (Disused)
Darl. Up Sdgs.
Dinsdale – CE Depot (Disused)
Stockton
Millfield–Thomson Scrap
Middlesbrough
Longbeck
Marske
Saltburn
Saltburn West Junc.

b
f
c Thornaby
(SEE INSET PAGE 69)
Marton

Whessoe Wks.
North Road
Darlington
d
a
1
Tees-side Airport
3
2
Eaglescliffe
Stockton Cut Junc.
CLEVELAND

Sdgs.
Dinsdale
Oak Tree Junc.
Allen's West
Eaglescliffe
Eaglescliffe S. Junc.
Gypsy Lane
Nunthorpe

Darlington S. Junc.

Great Ayton

*NORTH
YORKSHIRE*
Kildale
69

Battersby
B

Castle Hills Junc.
Northallerton East Junc.
Northallerton High Junc.

Finghall*
Northallerton

Boroughbridge Road Junc.
Longlands Junc.

Bedale*

1) Cleveland Bridge & Engineering Works
2) Naval Stores
3) Concrete Works – Dowmac
a) *Darlington North Junc.*
b) *Hopetown Junc.*
c) *Bowesfield Junc.*
d) *Parkgate Junc.*
e) *Seaton Snook Junc.*
f) *Hartburn Junc.*

Thirsk

C

0   5   10 m.

(1:350,000)

0   5   10   15   km.

1   2

68

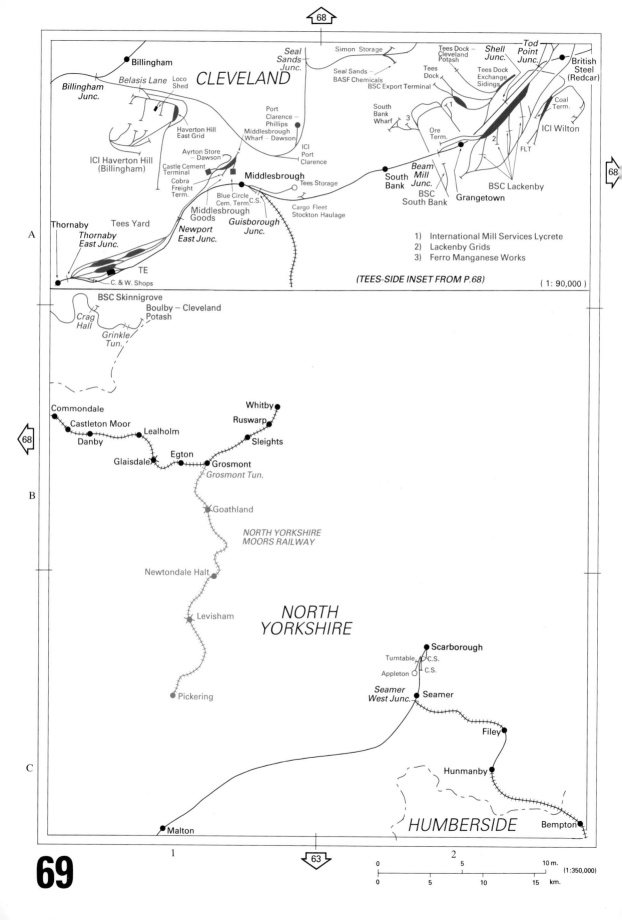

CLEVELAND

Billingham

Billingham Junc.

Belasis Lane Loco Shed

Seal Sands Junc.

Simon Storage

Seal Sands – BASF Chemicals

Tees Dock – Cleveland Potash

Shell Point Junc.

Tod Point Junc.

British Steel (Redcar)

Tees Dock

Tees Dock Exchange Sidings

BSC Export Terminal

Coal Term.

Haverton Hill East Grid

South Bank Wharf

ICI Wilton

Port Clarence – Phillips Middlesbrough Wharf – Dawson

ICI Port Clarence

Ore Term.

FLT

ICI Haverton Hill (Billingham)

Ayrton Store – Dawson

Castle Cement Terminal

Blue Circle Cem. Term.

Middlesbrough

Tees Storage

Beam Mill Junc.

Cobra Freight Term.

C.S.

Cargo Fleet Stockton Haulage

South Bank

BSC Lackenby

Thornaby

Tees Yard

Thornaby East Junc.

Middlesbrough Goods

Newport East Junc.

Guisborough Junc.

BSC South Bank

Grangetown

TE

C. & W. Shops

1) International Mill Services Lycrete
2) Lackenby Grids
3) Ferro Manganese Works

(TEES-SIDE INSET FROM P.68)

(1: 90,000)

A

BSC Skinnigrove

Boulby – Cleveland Potash

Crag Hall

Grinkle Tun.

Commondale

Castleton Moor

Danby

Lealholm

Glaisdale

Egton

Grosmont

Grosmont Tun.

Whitby

Ruswarp

Sleights

Goathland

NORTH YORKSHIRE MOORS RAILWAY

B

Newtondale Halt

NORTH YORKSHIRE

Levisham

Pickering

Scarborough

Turntable

C.S.

Appleton

C.S.

Seamer West Junc.

Seamer

Filey

Hunmanby

C

Malton

HUMBERSIDE

Bempton

1

2

0   5   10 m.

(1:350,000)

0   5   10   15   km.

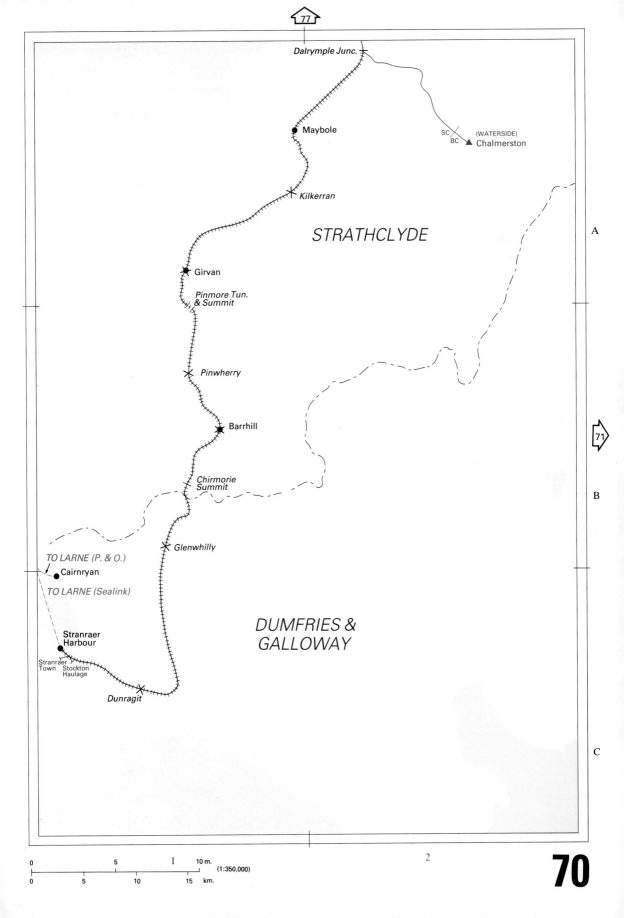

Dalrymple Junc.

Maybole

SC
BC
(WATERSIDE)
Chalmerston

Kilkerran

STRATHCLYDE

A

Girvan

Pinmore Tun.
& Summit

Pinwherry

Barrhill

71

Chirmorie
Summit

B

Glenwhilly

TO LARNE (P. & O.)
Cairnryan

TO LARNE (Sealink)

DUMFRIES &
GALLOWAY

Stranraer
Harbour

Stranraer
Town   Stockton
Haulage

Dunragit

C

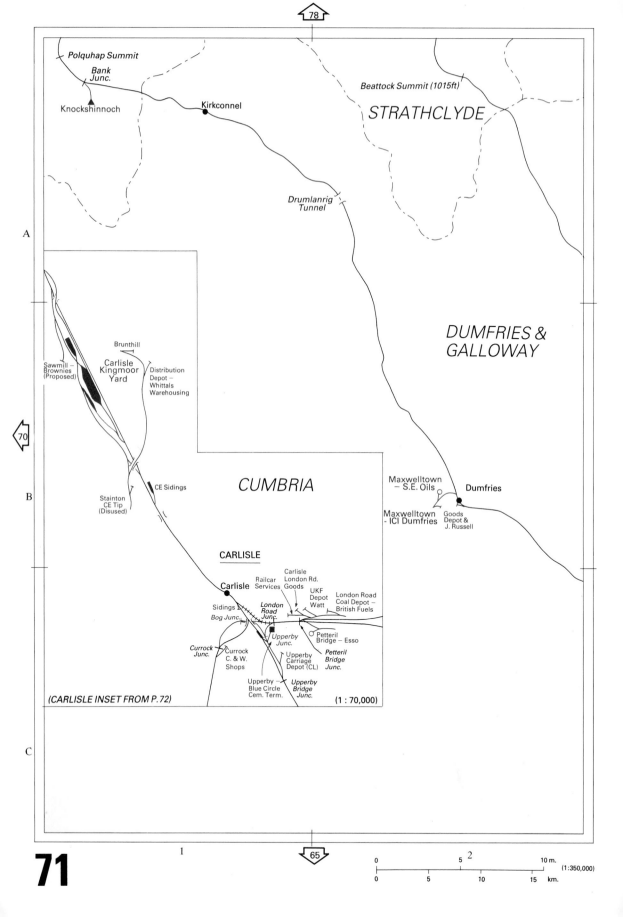

Polquhap Summit

Bank Junc.

Knockshinnoch

Kirkconnel

Beattock Summit (1015ft)

STRATHCLYDE

Drumlanrig Tunnel

A

DUMFRIES & GALLOWAY

70

Sawmill – Brownies (Proposed)

Brunthill

Carlisle Kingmoor Yard

Distribution Depot – Whittals Warehousing

CE Sidings

B

Stainton CE Tip (Disused)

CUMBRIA

Maxwelltown – S.E. Oils

Maxwelltown – ICI Dumfries

Dumfries

Goods Depot & J. Russell

CARLISLE

Carlisle

Railcar Services

Carlisle London Rd. Goods

UKF Depot Watt

London Road Coal Depot – British Fuels

Sidings

London Road Junc.

Bog Junc.

Upperby Junc.

Petteril Bridge – Esso

Currock Junc.

Currock C. & W. Shops

Upperby Carriage Depot (CL)

Petteril Bridge Junc.

Upperby – Blue Circle Cem. Term.

Upperby Bridge Junc.

(CARLISLE INSET FROM P. 72)

(1 : 70,000)

C

1

2

0   5   10 m.

(1:350,000)

0   5   10   15   km.

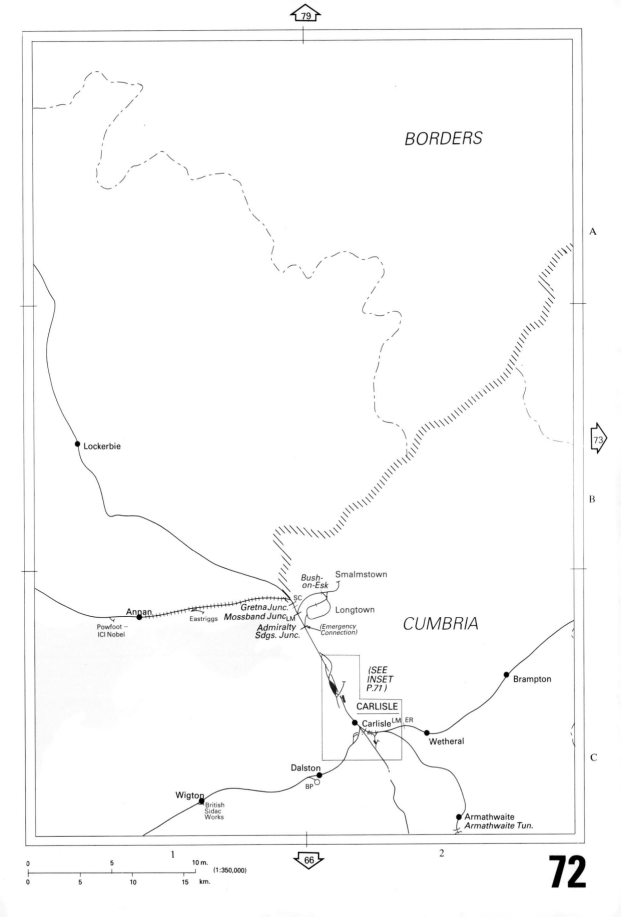

BORDERS

A

Lockerbie

73

B

Bush-
on-Esk   Smalmstown

SC

Annan   Gretna Junc.   Longtown   CUMBRIA
Eastriggs   Mossband Junc.LM
Powfoot –   Admiralty   (Emergency
ICI Nobel   Sdgs. Junc.   Connection)

(SEE
INSET   Brampton
P.71)

CARLISLE
Carlisle LM ER
Wetheral

C

Dalston
BP

Wigton
British   Armathwaite
Sidac   Armathwaite Tun.
Works

1   2

0   5   10 m.
(1:350,000)
0   5   10   15   km.

72

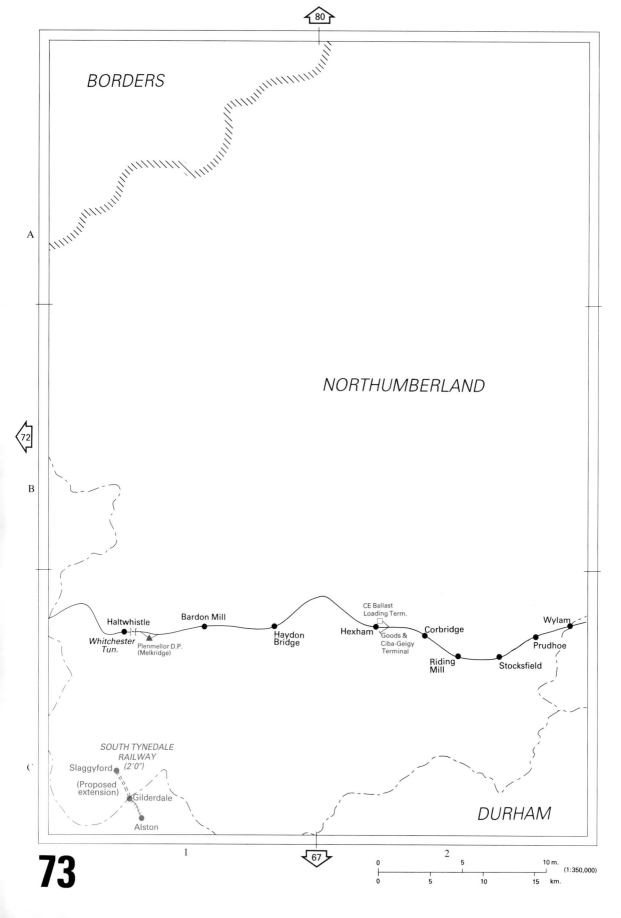

BORDERS

NORTHUMBERLAND

A

72

B

CE Ballast
Loading Term.

Wylam

Haltwhistle   Bardon Mill

Hexham   Corbridge

*Whitchester
Tun.*   Plenmellor D.P.
(Melkridge)   Haydon
Bridge   Goods &
Ciba-Geigy
Terminal   Riding
Mill   Prudhoe

Stocksfield

*SOUTH TYNEDALE
RAILWAY
(2'0")*

C   Slaggyford

(Proposed
extension)   Gilderdale

Alston

DURHAM

73

1   2

0   5   10 m.

(1:350,000)

0   5   10   15   km.

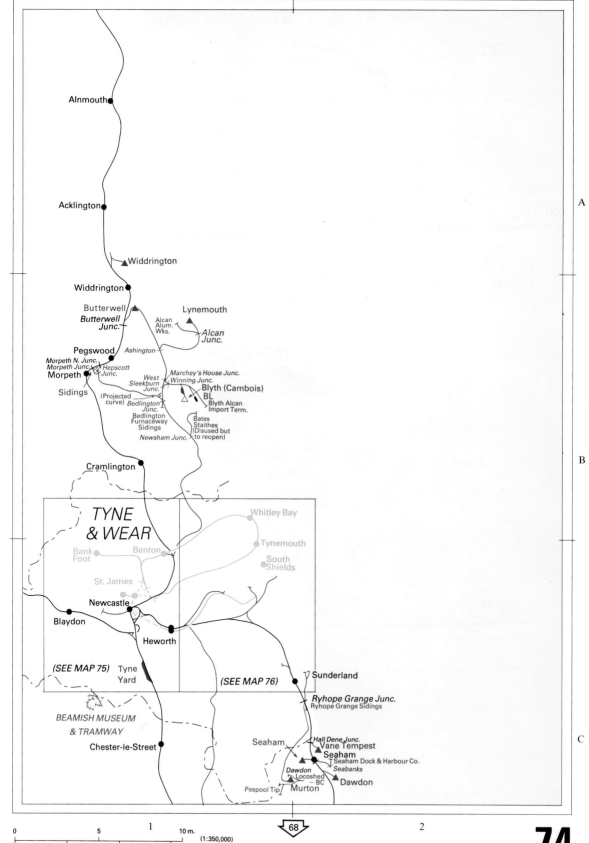

Alnmouth

Acklington

A

▲Widdrington

Widdrington

Butterwell
*Butterwell
Junc.*

Lynemouth ▲

Alcan
Alum.
Wks.

*Alcan
Junc.*

Pegswood

Ashington

Morpeth N. Junc.
Morpeth Junc. *Hepscott
Junc.*

Morpeth

Sidings

*West
Sleekburn
Junc.*

Marchey's House Junc.
Winning Junc.

Blyth (Cambois)
BL

Blyth Alcan
Import Term.

*(Projected
curve)*

*Bedlington
Junc.*

Bedlington
Furnaceway
Sidings

Newsham Junc.

Bates
Staithes
(Disused but
to reopen)

B

Cramlington

TYNE
& WEAR

Whitley Bay

Benton

Tynemouth

Bank
Foot

South
Shields

St. James

Newcastle

Blaydon

Heworth

(SEE MAP 75) Tyne
Yard

(SEE MAP 76)

Sunderland

Ryhope Grange Junc.
Ryhope Grange Sidings

BEAMISH MUSEUM
& TRAMWAY

Seaham

Hall Dene Junc.

Vane Tempest ▲

C

Chester-le-Street

Seaham
Seaham Dock & Harbour Co.
Seabanks

*Dawdon
Locoshed
BC*

Pespool Tip

Murton

Dawdon ▲

Dawdon

0   5   1   10 m.
0   5   10   15   km.   (1:350,000)

2

74

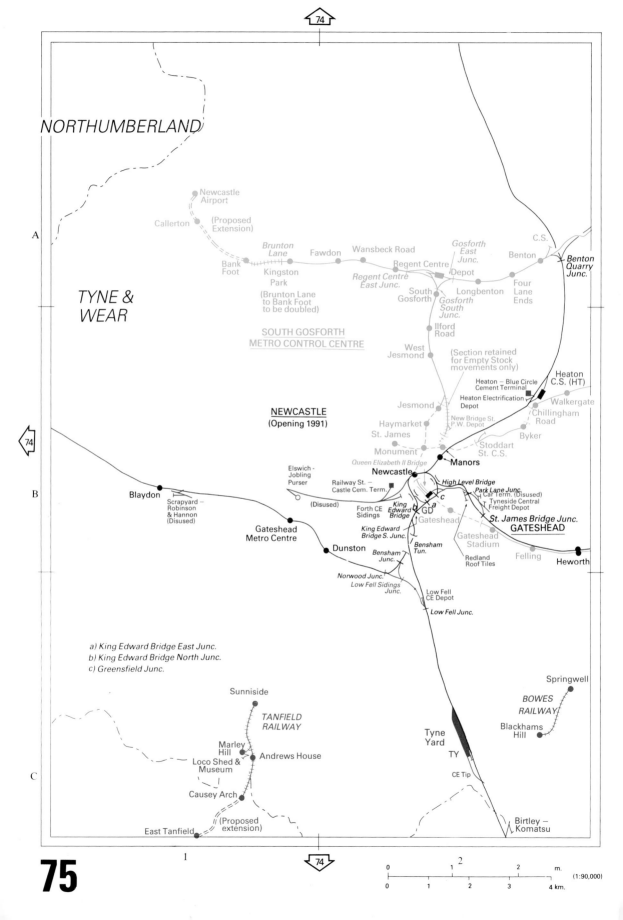

NORTHUMBERLAND

A

TYNE &
WEAR

Newcastle
Airport

Callerton

(Proposed
Extension)

Brunton
Lane

Fawdon

Wansbeck Road

Gosforth
East
Junc.

C.S.

Benton

Benton
Quarry
Junc.

Bank
Foot

Kingston
Park

(Brunton Lane
to Bank Foot
to be doubled)

Regent Centre

Regent Centre
East Junc.

South
Gosforth

Depot

Longbenton

Gosforth
South
Junc.

Four
Lane
Ends

SOUTH GOSFORTH
METRO CONTROL CENTRE

Ilford
Road

West
Jesmond

(Section retained
for Empty Stock
movements only)

NEWCASTLE
(Opening 1991)

Jesmond

Heaton – Blue Circle
Cement Terminal

Heaton Electrification
Depot

Heaton
C.S. (HT)

Walkergate

Haymarket

New Bridge St.
P.W. Depot

Chillingham
Road

St. James

Byker

Monument

Stoddart
St. C.S.

Elswich –
Jobling
Purser

Queen Elizabeth II Bridge

Manors

Railway St. –
Castle Cem. Term.

Newcastle

High Level Bridge

Park Lane Junc.

Blaydon

Scrapyard –
Robinson
& Hannon
(Disused)

(Disused)

Forth CE
Sidings

King
Edward
Bridge

GD

a

c

Gateshead

Car Term. (Disused)
Tyneside Central
Freight Depot

St. James Bridge Junc.

GATESHEAD

B

Gateshead
Metro Centre

Dunston

King Edward
Bridge S. Junc.

Bensham
Tun.

Gateshead
Stadium

Redland
Roof Tiles

Felling

Heworth

Bensham
Junc.

Norwood Junc.
Low Fell Sidings
Junc.

Low Fell
CE Depot

Low Fell Junc.

a) King Edward Bridge East Junc.
b) King Edward Bridge North Junc.
c) Greensfield Junc.

Springwell

Sunniside

TANFIELD
RAILWAY

BOWES
RAILWAY

Blackhams
Hill

Marley
Hill

Andrews House

Tyne
Yard

TY

Loco Shed &
Museum

Causey Arch

CE Tip

C

East Tanfield

(Proposed
extension)

Birtley –
Komatsu

1

2

0   1   2   m.

(1:90,000)

0   1   2   3   4 km.

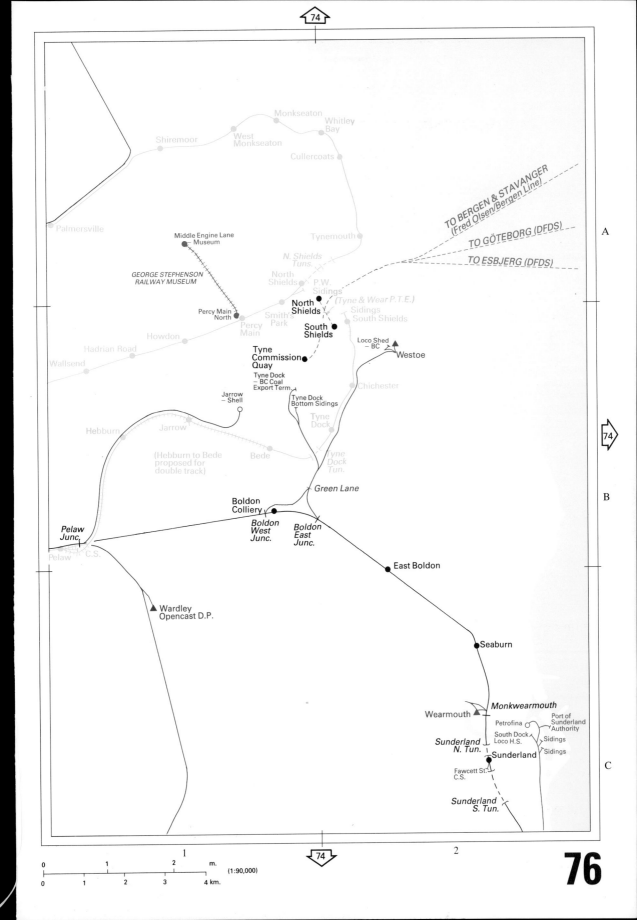

Monkseaton

Whitley
Bay

Shiremoor

West
Monkseaton

Cullercoats

Palmersville

Middle Engine Lane
— Museum

Tynemouth

TO BERGEN & STAVANGER
(Fred Olsen/Bergen Line)

TO GÖTEBORG (DFDS)

TO ESBJERG (DFDS)

*N. Shields
Tuns.*

*GEORGE STEPHENSON
RAILWAY MUSEUM*

North
Shields

P.W.
Sidings

(Tyne & Wear P.T.E.)

Percy Main
North

**North
Shields**

Sidings

South Shields

Smith's
Park

Percy Main

**South
Shields**

Loco Shed
– BC

Westoe

Howdon

Hadrian Road

Wallsend

**Tyne
Commission
Quay**

Tyne Dock
– BC Coal
Export Term.

Chichester

Jarrow
– Shell

Tyne Dock
Bottom Sidings

*Tyne
Dock*

Hebburn

Jarrow

(Hebburn to Bede
proposed for
double track)

Bede

*Tyne
Dock
Tun.*

Green Lane

**Boldon
Colliery**

*Boldon
West
Junc.*

*Boldon
East
Junc.*

*Pelaw
Junc.*

Pelaw   C.S.

East Boldon

▲ Wardley
Opencast D.P.

Seaburn

Wearmouth ▲

Monkwearmouth

Port of
Sunderland
Authority

Petrofina

South Dock
Loco H.S.

Sidings

Sidings

*Sunderland
N. Tun.*

Sunderland

Fawcett St.
C.S.

*Sunderland
S. Tun.*

1

2

0   1   2   m.

0   1   2   3   4 km.

(1:90,000)

Garelochhead
Luss

(Loch Lomond Marina Co.)

LOCH LOMOND

Helensburgh Upper
Helensburgh Central
Kilcreggan
Craigendoran
Craigendoran Junc.
Balloch Pier
Balloch
Alexandria

(Cal-Mac)
(Western Ferries)
(Clyde Marine)

Hunter's Quay
Gourock
Fort Matilda
Greenock West
Greenock Central
Cardross
Renton
Dalreoch Tuns.
Dalreoch

Dunoon
(Cal-Mac)
IBM Halt
Cartsdyke
James Watt Dock
Bogston
Dumbarton Cen.
Dumbarton East
Milngavie

COWAL
McInroy's Point
Branchton
Whinhill (Opens 1990)
Woodhall
Port Glasgow
No.2 Tun.
Bowling
(SEE MAP 81)

Dunrod
Inverkip
Inverkip Tun.
Langbank
British Aerospace
Bishopton No.1 Tun.
Dalmuir
Singer
Yoker

Wemyss Bay
Bishopton

a) Ladyburn Junc.
b) Wemyss Bay Junc.
c) Newton St. Tun. (1m 351yds)
d) Cartsburn Tun.
e) Ann St. Tun.
f) Wellpark Tun.

Paisley Gilmour St.
Johnstone
Milliken Park
Paisley Canal

Rothesay
ISLE OF BUTE

Cumbrae Slip
Largs
Barrhead
Neilston

ISLE OF GT. CUMBRAE
Millport
Gds
Fairlie Tun.
Fairlie
Lochwinnoch

Fairlie High – Hunterston Nuclear P.S.
Distribution Depot – Young
Glengarnock
Giffen
Distribution Depot – Lugton Property Co.
Lugton

Hunterston BSC Ore Reduction Plant
Hunterston Ore Terminal
West Kilbride
Dalry – Roche Products
Swinlees
Dunlop

(Cal-Mac)
Holm Junc.
Stewarton

STRATHCLYDE

Ardrossan South Beach
Kilwinning
Sdgs.
Dubbs Junc.
Byrehill Junc.

Ardrossan Harbour
ICI Snodgrass
J. Walker Distillery
Kilmaurs
S.E. Yard
Kilmarnock

(Cal-Mac)
TO BRODICK (ARRAN)
Ardrossan Town
Saltcoats
ICI Ardeer
Bogside Junc.
Kay Park Junc.
Barleith – J. Walker Distillery

Stevenston
Irvine
CE Depot
Blue Circle Cement Term. Goods
Riccarton – BP
Locomotive Works – A. Barclay

Irvine – Caledonian Paper
Shewalton CE Tip
Hillhouse
Meadowhead
Barassie
Barassie Junc.
Mossgiel Tun.
Mauchline Junc.

Heathfield (Projected)
Troon
(Reversing Spur)
Barassie CE Sidings

Falkland Yard
Ayr Harbour Junc.
SAI Works
Newton on-Ayr
Newton Junc.
Preswick – BP
Prestwick
Annbank Junc.

Ayr Harbour & Coal Terminal
Esso
AY
Heathfield (Projected)
Newton-on-Ayr
Auchincruive – Esso

Ayr
Townhead C.S.
(AYR INSET FROM RIGHT)
(1:90,000)
(SEE INSET TO LEFT)
Ayr
Auchinleck
Killoch Coll. (Ochiltree)

0 5 10 m. (1:350,000)
0 5 10 15 km.

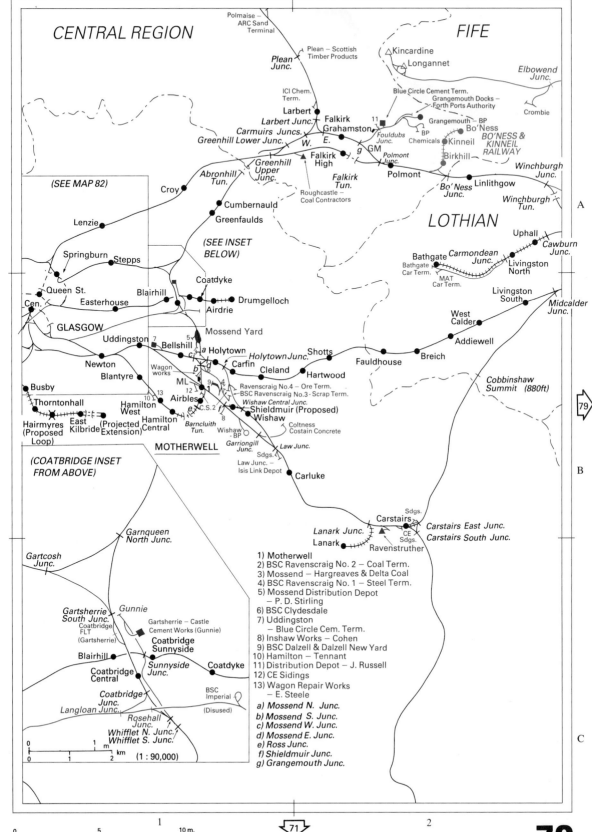

CENTRAL REGION

FIFE

Polmaise – ARC Sand Terminal

Plean – Scottish Timber Products

△ Kincardine
△ Longannet

Elbowend Junc.

Plean Junc.

Crombie

ICI Chem. Term.

Blue Circle Cement Term.
Grangemouth Docks – Forth Ports Authority

Larbert
Larbert Junc.
Carmuirs Juncs.
Greenhill Lower Junc.

Falkirk Grahamston

11

Grangemouth – BP
Bo'Ness

Fouldubs Junc.
BP Chemicals

Kinneil

BO'NESS & KINNEIL RAILWAY

W. E.
GM

Birkhill

▲ Falkirk High

Polmont Junc.

Greenhill Upper Junc.

Falkirk Tun.

g

Polmont

Linlithgow

Winchburgh Junc.

(SEE MAP 82)

Abronhill Tun.

Roughcastle – Coal Contractors

Bo' Ness Junc.

Winchburgh Tun.

A

Croy

Cumbernauld
Greenfaulds

LOTHIAN

Uphall
Cawburn Junc.

Lenzie

(SEE INSET BELOW)

Bathgate *Carmondean Junc.*
Bathgate Car Term.
MAT Car Term.

Livingston North

Springburn Stepps

Coatdyke

Livingston South

Midcalder Junc.

Queen St.
Cen.

Blairhill

Drumgelloch
Airdrie

West Calder

Easterhouse

Mossend Yard

Addiewell

GLASGOW

Uddingston
Bellshill

7
5
a Holytown

Shotts

Fauldhouse

Breich

Newton

c
b
d

Holytown Junc.

Carfin

Cleland

Hartwood

Busby

Blantyre

Wagon works

ML
12
9
4

Ravenscraig No.4 – Ore Term.
BSC Ravenscraig No.3 - Scrap Term.

Cobbinshaw Summit (880ft)

79

Thorntonhall

13
10

Airbles

Wishaw Central Junc.

Hairmyres (Proposed Loop)

East Kilbride

(Projected Extension)

Hamilton West
Hamilton Central

e
C.S.2
f
8

Shieldmuir (Proposed)
Wishaw

Barncluith Tun.

Coltness Costain Concrete

(COATBRIDGE INSET FROM ABOVE)

MOTHERWELL

Wishaw - BP

Garriongill Junc.

Law Junc.

B

Sdgs.
Law Junc. – Isis Link Depot

Carluke

Garnqueen North Junc.

Gartcosh Junc.

Carstairs

Sdgs.

Carstairs East Junc.
Carstairs South Junc.

Lanark Junc.

CE
Sdgs.

Lanark

Ravenstruther

Gunnie

Gartsherrie South Junc.
Coatbridge FLT (Gartsherrie)

Gartsherrie – Castle Cement Works (Gunnie)

Coatbridge Sunnyside

Blairhill

Coatbridge Central

Sunnyside Junc.

Coatdyke

BSC Imperial
(Disused)

Coatbridge Junc.
Langloan Junc.

Rosehall Junc.
Whifflet N. Junc.
Whifflet S. Junc.

1) Motherwell
2) BSC Ravenscraig No. 2 – Coal Term.
3) Mossend – Hargreaves & Delta Coal
4) BSC Ravenscraig No. 1 – Steel Term.
5) Mossend Distribution Depot
   – P. D. Stirling
6) BSC Clydesdale
7) Uddingston
   – Blue Circle Cem. Term.
8) Inshaw Works – Cohen
9) BSC Dalzell & Dalzell New Yard
10) Hamilton – Tennant
11) Distribution Depot – J. Russell
12) CE Sidings
13) Wagon Repair Works
    – E. Steele
a) *Mossend N. Junc.*
b) *Mossend S. Junc.*
c) *Mossend W. Junc.*
d) *Mossend E. Junc.*
e) *Ross Junc.*
f) *Shieldmuir Junc.*
g) *Grangemouth Junc.*

0   1   m
0   1   2   km

(1 : 90,000)

C

0   5   10 m.

(1:350,000)

0   5   10   15   km.

1

2

78

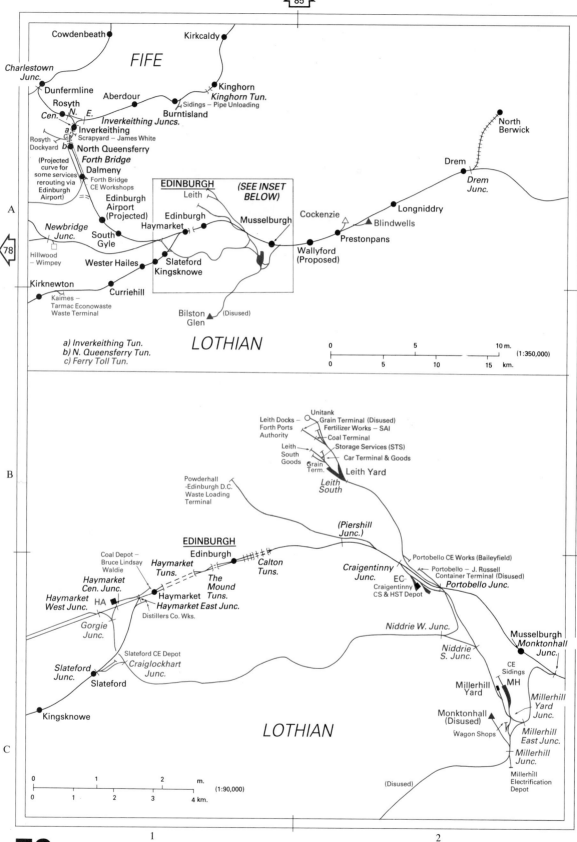

Cowdenbeath

Kirkcaldy

FIFE

Charlestown Junc.

Dunfermline
Aberdour
Rosyth
Cen.   N. E.
Kinghorn
Kinghorn Tun.
Burntisland
Sidings – Pipe Unloading

Inverkeithing Juncs.
a) Inverkeithing
Scrapyard – James White

Rosyth
Dockyard   b) North Queensferry

Forth Bridge

North Berwick

Drem
Drem Junc.

(Projected
curve for
some services
rerouting via
Edinburgh
Airport)

Dalmeny
Forth Bridge
CE Workshops

Edinburgh
Airport
(Projected)

EDINBURGH

Leith

(SEE INSET
BELOW)

Cockenzie

Longniddry

Blindwells

Edinburgh
Haymarket

Musselburgh

Newbridge
Junc.

South
Gyle

Prestonpans

Hillwood
– Wimpey

Wester Hailes

Slateford
Kingsknowe

Wallyford
(Proposed)

Kirknewton

Curriehill

Kaimes –
Tarmac Econowaste
Waste Terminal

Bilston
Glen   (Disused)

LOTHIAN

a) Inverkeithing Tun.
b) N. Queensferry Tun.
c) Ferry Toll Tun.

0		5		10 m.

(1:350,000)

0	5	10	15	km.

A

78

Unitank
Grain Terminal (Disused)
Leith Docks –
Forth Ports
Authority   Fertilizer Works – SAI
Coal Terminal
Leith   Storage Services (STS)
South
Goods   Car Terminal & Goods
Grain
Term.
Leith Yard
Leith
South

Powderhall
-Edinburgh D.C.
Waste Loading
Terminal

(Piershill
Junc.)

B

EDINBURGH

Coal Depot –
Bruce Lindsay
Waldie

Edinburgh

Haymarket
Tuns.

Calton
Tuns.

Portobello CE Works (Baileyfield)

Craigentinny
Junc.

EC

Portobello – J. Russell
Container Terminal (Disused)

Portobello Junc.

Haymarket
Cen. Junc.

The
Mound
Tuns.

Craigentinny
CS & HST Depot

Haymarket
West Junc.   HA

Haymarket
Haymarket East Junc.

Distillers Co. Wks.

Niddrie W. Junc.

Musselburgh
Monktonhall
Junc.

Gorgie
Junc.

Niddrie
S. Junc.

CE
Sidings

MH

Slateford CE Depot
Craiglockhart
Junc.

Millerhill
Yard

Millerhill
Yard
Junc.

Slateford
Junc.

Slateford

Monktonhall
(Disused)

Wagon Shops

Millerhill
East Junc.

Kingsknowe

Millerhill
Junc.

LOTHIAN

Millerhill
Electrification
Depot

(Disused)

0	1		2	m.

(1:90,000)

0	1	2	3	4 km.

C

1

2

79

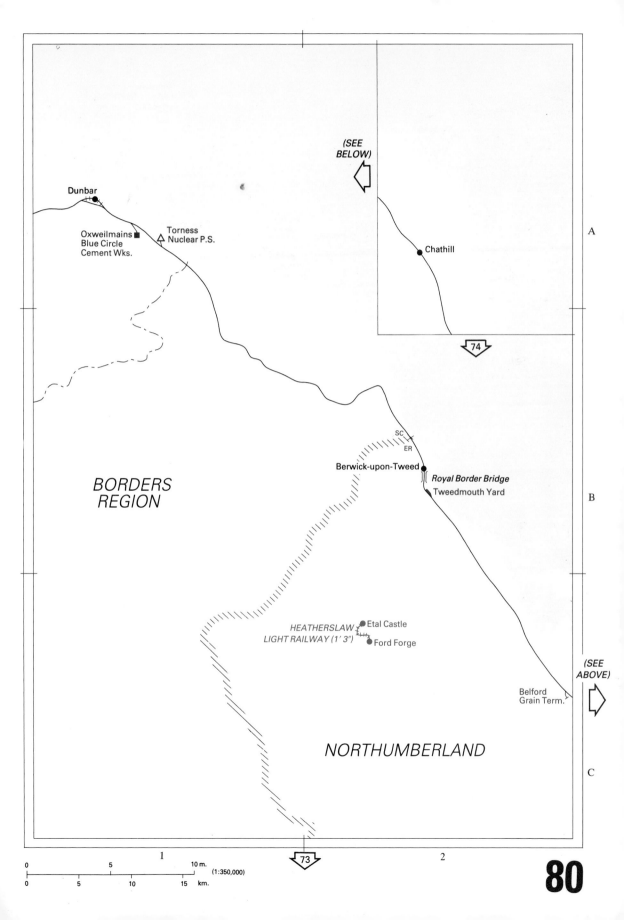

(SEE BELOW)

A

Chathill

74

Dunbar

Oxweilmains
Blue Circle
Cement Wks.

Torness
Nuclear P.S.

SC
ER

Berwick-upon-Tweed

Royal Border Bridge

Tweedmouth Yard

B

BORDERS
REGION

HEATHERSLAW
LIGHT RAILWAY (1' 3")

Etal Castle

Ford Forge

(SEE ABOVE)

Belford
Grain Term.

NORTHUMBERLAND

C

1   10 m.

(1:350,000)

0   5
0   5   10   15   km.

73

2

80

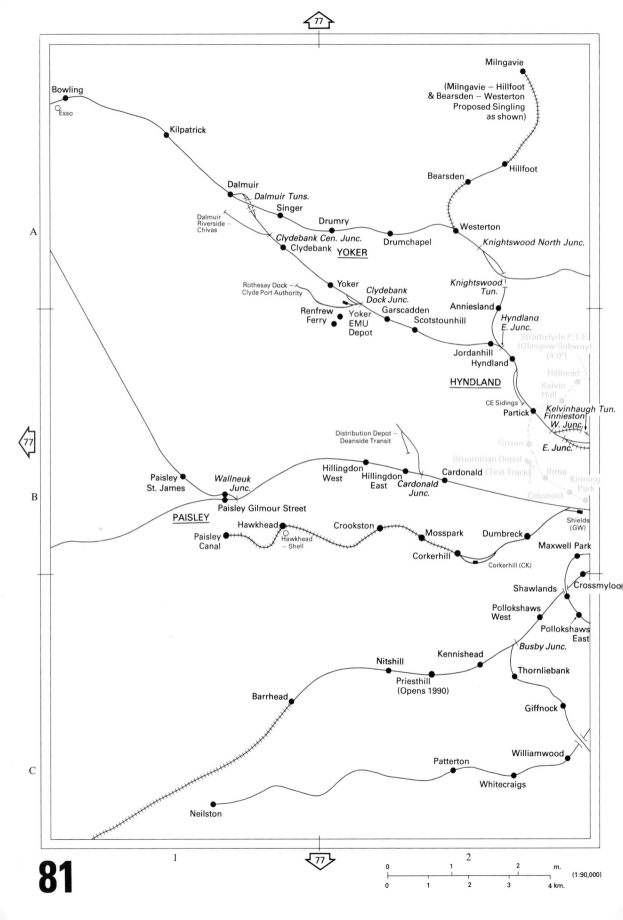

Milngavie

(Milngavie – Hillfoot
& Bearsden – Westerton
Proposed Singling
as shown)

Bowling

Esso

Kilpatrick

Hillfoot

Bearsden

Dalmuir

Dalmuir Tuns.

Singer

Westerton

Dalmuir
Riverside –
Chivas

Drumry

Knightswood North Junc.

YOKER

Clydebank Cen. Junc.
Clydebank

Drumchapel

A

Drumchapel

*Knightswood
Tun.*

Rothesay Dock –
Clyde Port Authority

Yoker

*Clydebank
Dock Junc.*

Knightswood
Tun.

Anniesland

Renfrew
Ferry

Yoker
EMU
Depot

Garscadden

Scotstounhill

*Hyndland
E. Junc.*

Strathclyde P.T.E.
(Glasgow Subway)
(4'0")

Jordanhill
Hyndland

Hillhead

Kelvin
Hall

HYNDLAND

CE Sidings

Kelvinhaugh Tun.
Partick   Finnieston
          W. Junc.

Distribution Depot –
Deanside Transit

Govan

Broomloan Depot
(Test Track)

E. Junc.

Ibrox

Hillingdon
West

Hillingdon
East

Cardonald

Kinning
Park

Paisley
St. James

*Wallneuk
Junc.*

*Cardonald
Junc.*

Cessnock

B

Paisley Gilmour Street

Shields
(GW)

PAISLEY

Hawkhead

Crookston

Dumbreck

Maxwell Park

Paisley
Canal

Hawkhead –
Shell

Mosspark

Corkerhill

Corkerhill (CK)

Shawlands

Crossmyloo

Pollokshaws
West

Pollokshaws
East

Kennishead

Busby Junc.

Nitshill

Thornliebank

Barrhead

Priesthill
(Opens 1990)

Giffnock

Williamwood

C

Patterton

Whitecraigs

Neilston

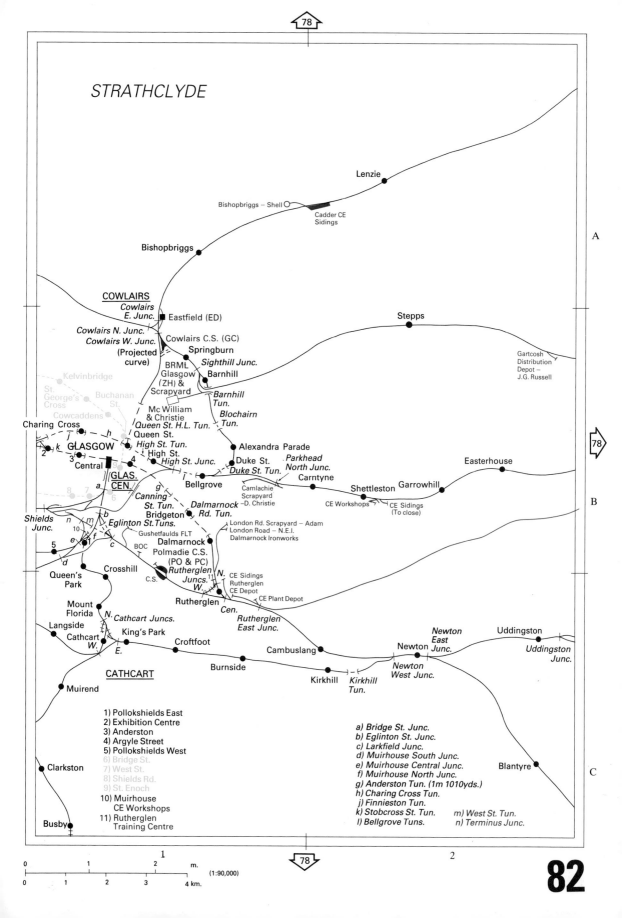

STRATHCLYDE

Lenzie

Bishopbriggs – Shell

Cadder CE
Sidings

A

Bishopbriggs

COWLAIRS
Cowlairs
E. Junc.   Eastfield (ED)
Cowlairs N. Junc.
Cowlairs W. Junc.   Cowlairs C.S. (GC)
(Projected   Springburn
curve)   Sighthill Junc.
BRML   Barnhill
Glasgow
(ZH) &   Barnhill
Scrapyard   Tun.
Mc William   Blochairn
& Christie   Tun.
Queen St. H.L. Tun.
Queen St.
High St. Tun.   Alexandra Parade
High St.
Central   High St. Junc.   Duke St.
                 Duke St. Tun.   Parkhead
GLAS.   North Junc.
CEN.   Bellgrove
Canning   Camlachie
St. Tun.   Scrapyard
Bridgeton   –D. Christie
Eglinton St.Tuns. Dalmarnock
                 Rd. Tun.
Shields   London Rd. Scrapyard – Adam
Junc.   London Road – N.E.I.
                 Dalmarnock Ironworks
                 Dalmarnock
BOC   Polmadie C.S.
                 (PO & PC)
                 Rutherglen
C.S.   Juncs.
Queen's   Rutherglen
Park   Cen.
Crosshill
Mount   Rutherglen
Florida   East Junc.
Langside   N. Cathcart Juncs.
Cathcart   King's Park
W.   Croftfoot   Cambuslang
E.
CATHCART   Burnside
Muirend   Kirkhill
                                  Kirkhill
                                  Tun.

Stepps

Gartcosh
Distribution
Depot –
J.G. Russell

Easterhouse

78   B

Carntyne
Shettleston   Garrowhill
CE Workshops CE Sidings
              (To close)

CE Sidings
Rutherglen
CE Depot
CE Plant Depot

Newton
East
Junc.   Uddingston

Newton   Uddingston
             Junc.
Newton
West Junc.

Kelvinbridge
St.
George's
Cross   Buchanan
Cowcaddens   St.
Charing Cross
GLASGOW
Central

Blantyre   C

Clarkston

Busby

1) Pollokshields East
2) Exhibition Centre
3) Anderston
4) Argyle Street
5) Pollokshields West
6) Bridge St.
7) West St.
8) Shields Rd.
9) St. Enoch
10) Muirhouse
    CE Workshops
11) Rutherglen
    Training Centre

a) Bridge St. Junc.
b) Eglinton St. Junc.
c) Larkfield Junc.
d) Muirhouse South Junc.
e) Muirhouse Central Junc.
f) Muirhouse North Junc.
g) Anderston Tun. (1m 1010yds.)
h) Charing Cross Tun.
j) Finnieston Tun.
k) Stobcross St. Tun.   m) West St. Tun.
l) Bellgrove Tuns.   n) Terminus Junc.

1   2

0   1   2   m.
0   1   2   3   4 km.
(1:90,000)

82

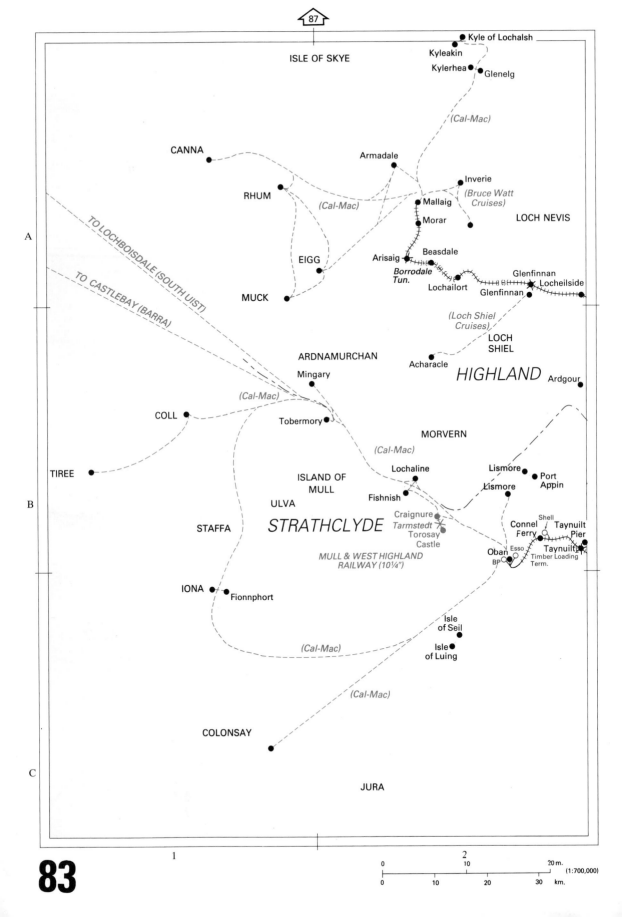

Kyle of Lochalsh
Kyleakin
Kylerhea
Glenelg

ISLE OF SKYE

(Cal-Mac)

CANNA

Armadale

Inverie

(Bruce Watt
Cruises)

RHUM

Mallaig

LOCH NEVIS

(Cal-Mac)

Morar

EIGG

Beasdale

A

Arisaig

Borrodale
Tun.

Glenfinnan
Locheilside

Lochailort

Glenfinnan

MUCK

(Loch Shiel
Cruises)

LOCH
SHIEL

ARDNAMURCHAN

Acharacle

HIGHLAND

Mingary

Ardgour

(Cal-Mac)

COLL

Tobermory

MORVERN

(Cal-Mac)

Lochaline

Lismore
Port
Appin

TIREE

ISLAND OF
MULL

Lismore

B

ULVA

Fishnish

STAFFA

STRATHCLYDE

Craignure
Tarmstedt
Torosay
Castle

Shell
Connel
Ferry
Taynuilt
Pier

Esso

Taynuilt

Oban
BP

Timber Loading
Term.

MULL & WEST HIGHLAND
RAILWAY (10¼")

IONA

Fionnphort

Isle
of Seil

Isle
of Luing

(Cal-Mac)

(Cal-Mac)

COLONSAY

C

JURA

TO LOCHBOISDALE (SOUTH UIST)

TO CASTLEBAY (BARRA)

1

2

0   10   20 m.

(1:700,000)

0   10   20   30   km.

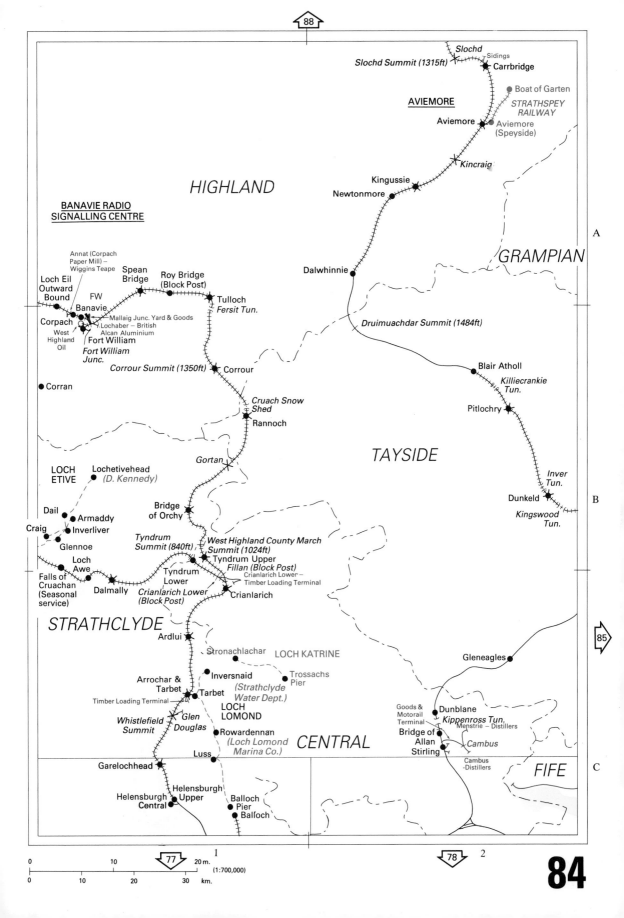

Slochd

Slochd Summit (1315ft) — Sidings
★ Carrbridge

● Boat of Garten

AVIEMORE *STRATHSPEY RAILWAY*

★ Aviemore
Aviemore (Speyside)

★ *Kincraig*

HIGHLAND

Kingussie ★
Newtonmore ●

A

GRAMPIAN

● Dalwhinnie

**BANAVIE RADIO
SIGNALLING CENTRE**

Druimuachdar Summit (1484ft)

Annat (Corpach
Paper Mill) —
Wiggins Teape

Spean ★
Bridge
Roy Bridge
(Block Post)

● Tulloch
Fersit Tun.

Loch Eil
Outward
Bound
FW
Banavie
Corpach
West
Highland
Oil
—Mallaig Junc. Yard & Goods
Lochaber — British
Alcan Aluminium
Fort William
*Fort William
Junc.*

● Blair Atholl

*Killiecrankie
Tun.*

Corrour Summit (1350ft) ★ Corrour

Pitlochry ★

● Corran

*Cruach Snow
Shed*
Rannoch

TAYSIDE

Gortan

*Inver
Tun.*

**LOCH
ETIVE**
Lochetivehead
(D. Kennedy)

Dunkeld ★
B

Bridge
of Orchy

*Kingswood
Tun.*

Dail ●
● Armaddy
Craig ●
Inverliver
Glennoe ●

*Tyndrum
Summit (840ft)*
*West Highland County March
Summit (1024ft)*
Tyndrum Upper
Fillan (Block Post)
Crianlarich Lower —
Timber Loading Terminal

Loch
Awe
Tyndrum
Lower
Falls of
Cruachan
(Seasonal
service)
Dalmally
*Crianlarich Lower
(Block Post)*
Crianlarich

STRATHCLYDE

Ardlui ★

Gleneagles ●

Stronachlachar ●   **LOCH KATRINE**

Inversnaid
● Trossachs
Pier

Arrochar &
Tarbet
Tarbet
*(Strathclyde
Water Dept.)*

Goods &
Motorail
Terminal
Dunblane ●
Kippenross Tun.
Menstrie — Distillers

Timber Loading Terminal

*Whistlefield
Summit*
**Glen
Douglas**

**LOCH
LOMOND**

Bridge of
Allan
Stirling
Cambus

Rowardennan
*(Loch Lomond
Marina Co.)*

CENTRAL

Cambus
-Distillers

Luss ●

FIFE
C

Garelochhead ★

Helensburgh
Upper
Balloch
Pier
Helensburgh
Central
Balloch

0 ——— 10 ——— 20 m.
0 — 10 — 20 — 30 km.
(1:700,000)

1

77

2

78

85

84

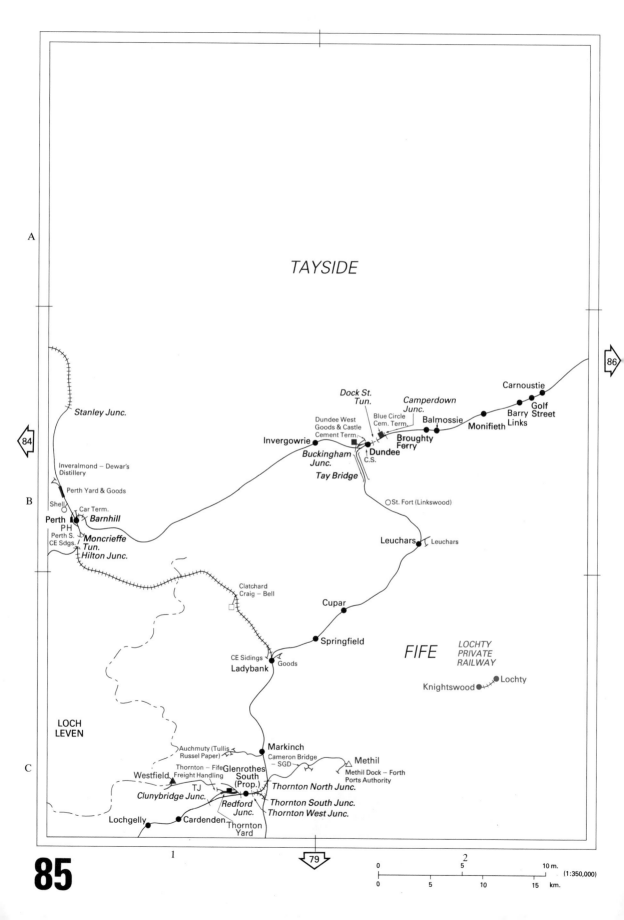

TAYSIDE

FIFE

LOCHTY
PRIVATE
RAILWAY

LOCH
LEVEN

A

B

C

1   2

Stanley Junc.

Inveralmond – Dewar's
Distillery

Perth Yard & Goods

Shell
Perth
PH
Perth S.
CE Sdgs.

Car Term.

Barnhill

*Moncrieffe
Tun.*

Hilton Junc.

*Dock St.
Tun.*

*Camperdown
Junc.*

Dundee West
Goods & Castle
Cement Term.

Blue Circle
Cem. Term.

Carnoustie

Golf
Street

Barry
Links

Monifieth

Balmossie

Broughty
Ferry

Invergowrie

*Buckingham
Junc.*

Dundee
C.S.

Tay Bridge

○ St. Fort (Linkswood)

Leuchars   Leuchars

Clatchard
Craig – Bell

Cupar

Springfield

CE Sidings

Ladybank   Goods

Knightswood ●━━━● Lochty

Auchmuty (Tullis
Russel Paper)

Markinch

Cameron Bridge
SGD

△ Methil

Methil Dock – Forth
Ports Authority

Westfield

Thornton – Fife
Freight Handling

Glenrothes
South
(Prop.)

TJ

Clunybridge Junc.

*Redford
Junc.*

Thornton North Junc.

Thornton South Junc.

Thornton West Junc.

Lochgelly   Cardenden

Thornton
Yard

84

86

79

0   5   10 m.

0   5   10   15   km.

(1:350,000)

85

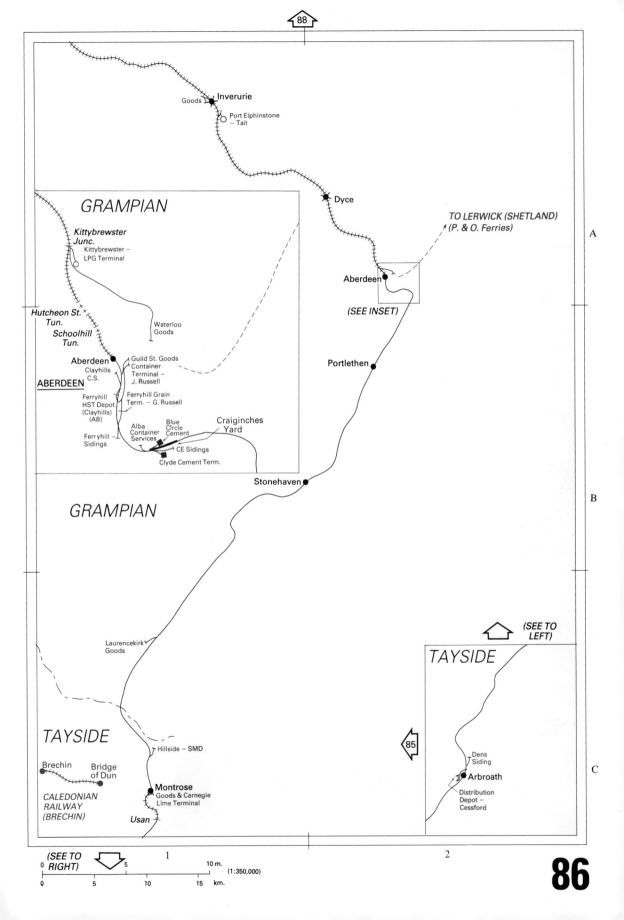

Goods

Inverurie

Port Elphinstone
– Tait

Dyce

TO LERWICK (SHETLAND)
(P. & O. Ferries)

A

Aberdeen

(SEE INSET)

GRAMPIAN

Kittybrewster
Junc.
Kittybrewster –
LPG Terminal

Hutcheon St.
Tun.
Schoolhill
Tun.

Waterloo
Goods

Aberdeen

ABERDEEN

Guild St. Goods
Clayhills   Container
C.S.   Terminal –
               J. Russell

Ferryhill   Ferryhill Grain
HST Depot   Term. – G. Russell
(Clayhills)
(AB)

               Blue   *Craiginches*
Alba   Circle   *Yard*
Container   Cement
Services

Ferryhill   CE Sidings
Sidings
               Clyde Cement Term.

Portlethen

Stonehaven

B

GRAMPIAN

Laurencekirk
Goods

(SEE TO
LEFT)

TAYSIDE

85

TAYSIDE

Hillside – SMD

Dens
Siding

Brechin   **Bridge**
             of Dun

Montrose
Goods & Carnegie
Lime Terminal

CALEDONIAN
RAILWAY
(BRECHIN)

Usan

Arbroath

Distribution
Depot –
Cessford

C

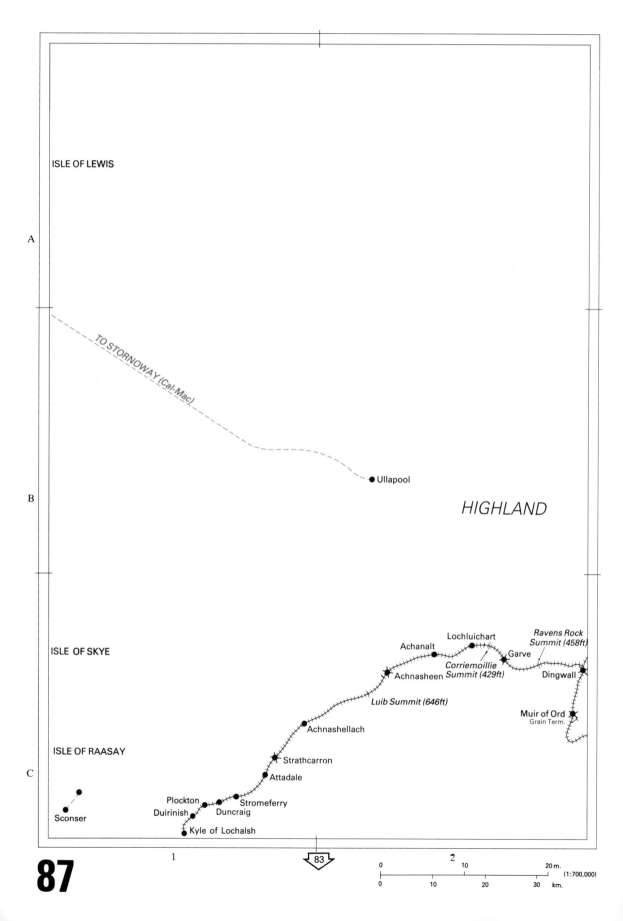

ISLE OF LEWIS

A

TO STORNOWAY (Cal-Mac)

● Ullapool

HIGHLAND

B

ISLE OF SKYE

Lochluichart

Ravens Rock Summit (458ft)

Achanalt

Garve

Corriemoillie Summit (429ft)

Achnasheen

Dingwall

Luib Summit (646ft)

Achnashellach

Muir of Ord
Grain Term.

ISLE OF RAASAY

Strathcarron

C

Attadale

Plockton

Stromeferry

Duirinish

Duncraig

Sconser

Kyle of Lochalsh

1

83

2

0   10   20 m.
(1:700,000)
0   10   20   30   km.

87

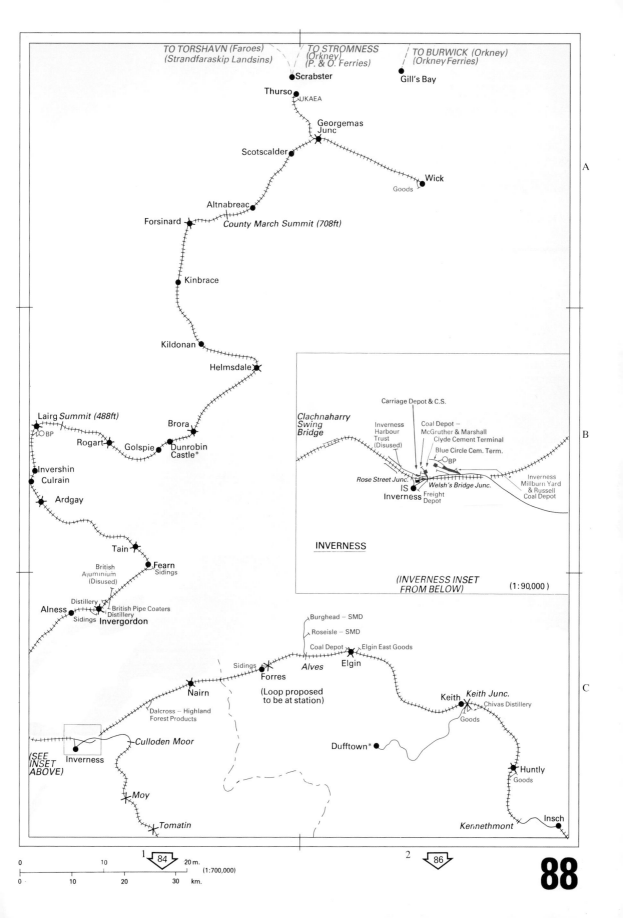

TO TORSHAVN (Faroes)
(Strandfaraskip Landsins)

TO STROMNESS (Orkney)
(P. & O. Ferries)

TO BURWICK (Orkney)
(Orkney Ferries)

● Scrabster

● Gill's Bay

Thurso ●
UKAEA

Georgemas Junc

Scotscalder ●

Wick ●
Goods

Altnabreac ●

Forsinard ★   *County March Summit (708ft)*

Kinbrace ●

Kildonan ●

Helmsdale ●

Lairg *Summit (488ft)*
○ BP

Brora ★

Rogart

Golspie ●   Dunrobin Castle*

● Invershin
● Culrain

★ Ardgay

Tain ●

Fearn ● Sidings

British Aluminium (Disused)

Distillery
Alness ●   British Pipe Coaters Distillery
Sidings   **Invergordon**

INVERNESS INSET

Carriage Depot & C.S.

Clachnaharry Swing Bridge

Inverness Harbour Trust (Disused)

Coal Depot – McGruther & Marshall
Clyde Cement Terminal
Blue Circle Cem. Term.
○ BP

Rose Street Junc.

IS
Inverness   *Welsh's Bridge Junc.*
Freight Depot

Inverness Millburn Yard & Russell Coal Depot

INVERNESS

(INVERNESS INSET FROM BELOW)   (1:90,000)

Burghead – SMD
Roseisle – SMD
Coal Depot   ● Elgin East Goods
Sidings   *Alves*   ★ Elgin

Keith *Keith Junc.*
Chivas Distillery
Goods

Forres
(Loop proposed to be at station)

Nairn ★
Dalcross – Highland Forest Products

Dufftown* ●

★ Huntly
Goods

Culloden Moor

(SEE INSET ABOVE)
● Inverness

✕ *Moy*

✕ *Tomatin*

Kennethmont   ● Insch

0   10   20 m.
1 ▽ 84   (1:700,000)
0   10   20   30 km.

2 ▽ 86

88

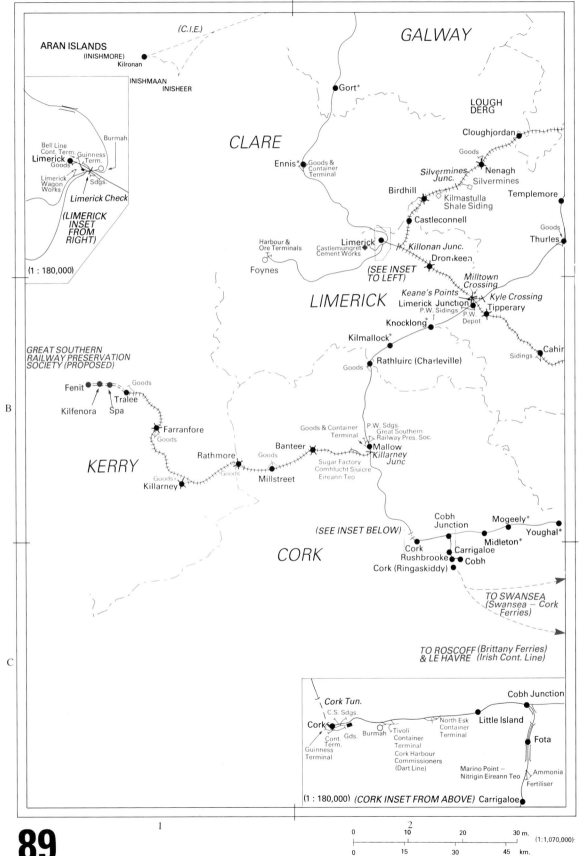

ARAN ISLANDS
(INISHMORE)
Kilronan

INISHMAAN
INISHEER

(C.I.E.)

GALWAY

Gort*

LOUGH DERG

CLARE

Cloughjordan

Ennis* Goods & Container Terminal

Goods

Silvermines Junc. Nenagh
Silvermines

Birdhill

Templemore

Kilmastulla Shale Siding

Castleconnell

Goods

Harbour & Ore Terminals Limerick
Castlemungret Cement Works Killonan Junc.

Thurles

Foynes

(SEE INSET TO LEFT)

Dromkeen

Milltown Crossing

LIMERICK

Keane's Points
Limerick Junction
P.W. Sidings

Kyle Crossing
Tipperary

Knocklong*

P.W. Depot

Kilmallock*

Rathluirc (Charleville)

Cahir

Sidings

Goods

GREAT SOUTHERN
RAILWAY PRESERVATION
SOCIETY (PROPOSED)

Fenit Goods
Tralee
Kilfenora Spa

B

Farranfore
Goods

Rathmore

Banteer

Goods & Container Terminal

P.W. Sdgs.
Great Southern
Railway Pres. Soc.

KERRY

Goods

Goods

Millstreet

Mallow

Killarney Junc

Killarney

Sugar Factory
Comhlucht Siuicre
Eireann Teo

Cobh Junction

Mogeely*
Youghal*

Midleton*

(SEE INSET BELOW)

CORK

Cork
Rushbrooke
Cork (Ringaskiddy)

Carrigaloe
Cobh

TO SWANSEA
(Swansea – Cork
Ferries)

TO ROSCOFF (Brittany Ferries)
& LE HAVRE (Irish Cont. Line)

C

LIMERICK INSET:

Bell Line
Cont. Term. Burmah
Limerick Guinness
Goods Term.

Limerick
Wagon
Works Sdgs.

Limerick Check

(LIMERICK
INSET
FROM
RIGHT)

(1 : 180,000)

CORK INSET:

Cork Tun.

C.S. Sdgs.

North Esk
Container
Terminal

Cobh Junction

Cork Burmah Little Island

Cont. Gds.
Term.
Guinness
Terminal

Tivoli
Container
Terminal
Cork Harbour
Commissioners
(Dart Line)

Fota

Marino Point –
Nitrigin Eireann Teo

Ammonia

Fertiliser

(1:180,000) (CORK INSET FROM ABOVE) Carrigaloe

89

1

2
0   10   20   30 m.
(1:1,070,000)
0   15   30   45 km.

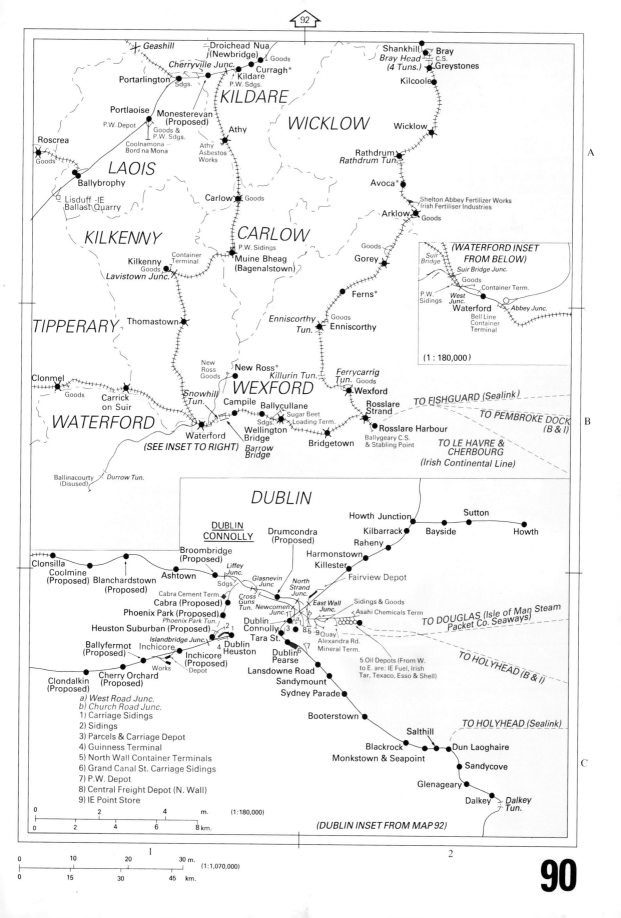

Geashill
Droichead Nua (Newbridge)
Goods
Cherryville Junc.
Curragh*
Portarlington
Kildare
P.W. Sdgs.
Sdgs.
KILDARE
Shankhill
Bray
Bray Head (4 Tuns.)
C.S.
Greystones
Kilcoole
Portlaoise
Monesterevan (Proposed)
P.W. Depot
Goods & P.W. Sdgs.
Athy
WICKLOW
Wicklow
Roscrea
Coolnamona – Bord na Mona
A
Goods
LAOIS
Rathdrum
Rathdrum Tun.
Ballybrophy
Athy Asbestos Works
Avoca*
Lisduff -IE Ballast Quarry
Carlow
Goods
Arklow
Shelton Abbey Fertilizer Works
Irish Fertiliser Industries
KILKENNY
CARLOW
Goods

(WATERFORD INSET FROM BELOW)
Suir Bridge
Suir Bridge Junc.
Goods
Container Term.
P.W. Sidings
West Junc.
Waterford
Abbey Junc.
Bell Line Container Terminal
(1 : 180,000)

Kilkenny
Goods
Container Terminal
Lavistown Junc.
P.W. Sidings
Muine Bheag (Bagenalstown)
Goods
Gorey
Goods
Ferns*

TIPPERARY
Thomastown
Enniscorthy Tun.
Goods
Enniscorthy

Clonmel
Goods
New Ross Goods
New Ross*
Killurin Tun.
Ferrycarrig Tun.
Goods
Wexford
TO FISHGUARD (Sealink)
Carrick on Suir
Snowhill Tun.
WEXFORD
Campile
Ballycullane
Rosslare Strand
TO PEMBROKE DOCK (B & I)
B
WATERFORD
Waterford
(SEE INSET TO RIGHT)
Wellington Bridge
Barrow Bridge
Sugar Beet Loading Term.
Bridgetown
Rosslare Harbour
Ballygeary C.S. & Stabling Point
TO LE HAVRE & CHERBOURG
(Irish Continental Line)

Ballinacourty (Disused)
Durrow Tun.

DUBLIN
Howth Junction
Sutton
DUBLIN CONNOLLY
Drumcondra (Proposed)
Kilbarrack
Bayside
Howth
Broombridge (Proposed)
Raheny
Clonsilla
Coolmine (Proposed)
Blanchardstown (Proposed)
Ashtown
Liffey Junc.
Sdgs.
Glasnevin Junc.
North Strand Junc.
Harmonstown
Killester
Fairview Depot
Cabra Cement Term.
Cabra (Proposed)
Cross Guns Tun.
Newcomen Junc.
East Wall Junc.
Sidings & Goods
Asahi Chemicals Term
Phoenix Park (Proposed)
Phoenix Park Tun.
Dublin Connolly
TO DOUGLAS (Isle of Man Steam Packet Co. Seaways)
Heuston Suburban (Proposed)
Islandbridge Junc.
Dublin Heuston
Tara St.
Alexandra Rd. Mineral Term.
Ballyfermot (Proposed)
Inchicore
Inchicore (Proposed)
Works
Depot
Dublin Pearse
TO HOLYHEAD (B & I)
Cherry Orchard (Proposed)
Lansdowne Road
5 Oil Depots (From W. to E. are: IE Fuel, Irish Tar, Texaco, Esso & Shell)
Clondalkin (Proposed)
Sandymount
Sydney Parade
a) West Road Junc.
b) Church Road Junc.
1) Carriage Sidings
2) Sidings
3) Parcels & Carriage Depot
4) Guinness Terminal
5) North Wall Container Terminals
6) Grand Canal St. Carriage Sidings
7) P.W. Depot
8) Central Freight Depot (N. Wall)
9) IE Point Store
Booterstown
Salthill
TO HOLYHEAD (Sealink)
Blackrock
Dun Laoghaire
Monkstown & Seapoint
Sandycove
Glenageary
Dalkey
Dalkey Tun.
C

0   2   4   m.   (1:180,000)
0   2   4   6   8 km.
(DUBLIN INSET FROM MAP 92)

0   10   20   30 m.
(1:1,070,000)
0   15   30   45 km.

1
2

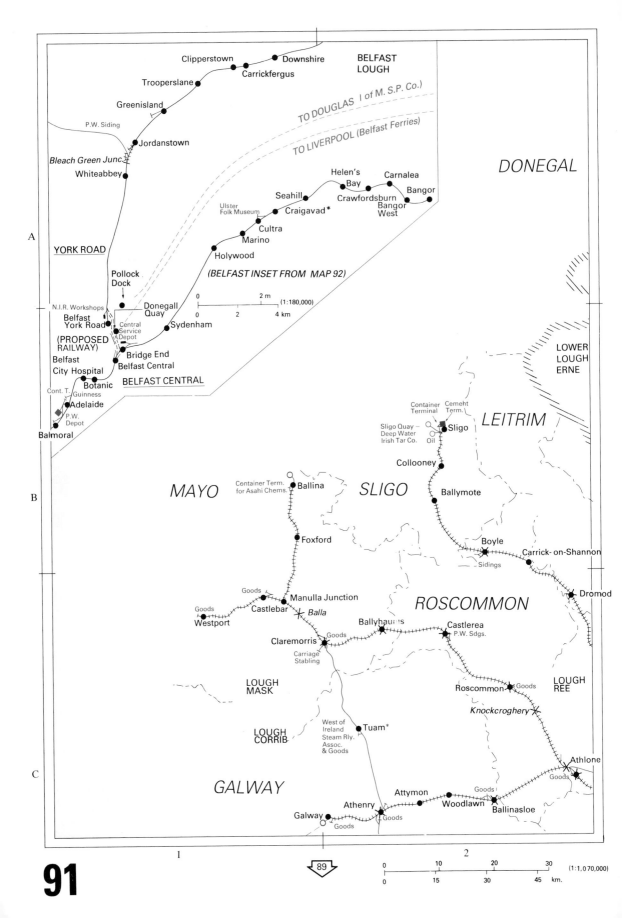

Clipperstown
Downshire
BELFAST
LOUGH
Carrickfergus
Trooperslane
Greenisland
P.W. Siding
DONEGAL
TO DOUGLAS I of M. S.P. Co.
TO LIVERPOOL (Belfast Ferries)
Jordanstown
Bleach Green Junc.
Whiteabbey
Helen's
Bay
Carnalea
Seahill
Crawfordsburn
Bangor
Ulster
Folk Museum
Craigavad*
Bangor
West
Cultra
A
Marino
YORK ROAD
Holywood
(BELFAST INSET FROM MAP 92)

0   2 m
(1:180,000)
0   2   4 km

Pollock
Dock
N.I.R. Workshops
Donegall
Quay
Belfast
York Road
Sydenham
Central
Service
Depot
*(PROPOSED
RAILWAY)*
Bridge End
Belfast Central
Belfast
City Hospital
BELFAST CENTRAL
Botanic
Cont. T. Guinness
Adelaide
*P.W.
Depot*
Balmoral

Container
Terminal
Cement
Term.
Sligo Quay –
Deep Water
Irish Tar Co.
Sligo
LEITRIM
Oil
LOWER
LOUGH
ERNE

Collooney

B
MAYO
Container Term.
for Asahi Chems.
Ballina
SLIGO
Ballymote

Foxford
Boyle
Carrick-on-Shannon
Sidings
ROSCOMMON
Dromod
Goods
Manulla Junction
Castlebar
Balla
Goods
Westport
Ballyhaunis
Castlerea
P.W. Sdgs.
Claremorris
Goods
LOUGH
MASK
Carriage
Stabling
Roscommon
Goods
LOUGH
REE

Knockcroghery
LOUGH
CORRIB
West of
Ireland
Steam Rly.
Assoc.
& Goods
Tuam*
Athlone
C
Goods
GALWAY
Attymon
Goods
Galway
Athenry
Woodlawn
Ballinasloe
Goods
Goods

1   89   2

0   10   20   30
(1:1,070,000)
0   15   30   45   km.

91

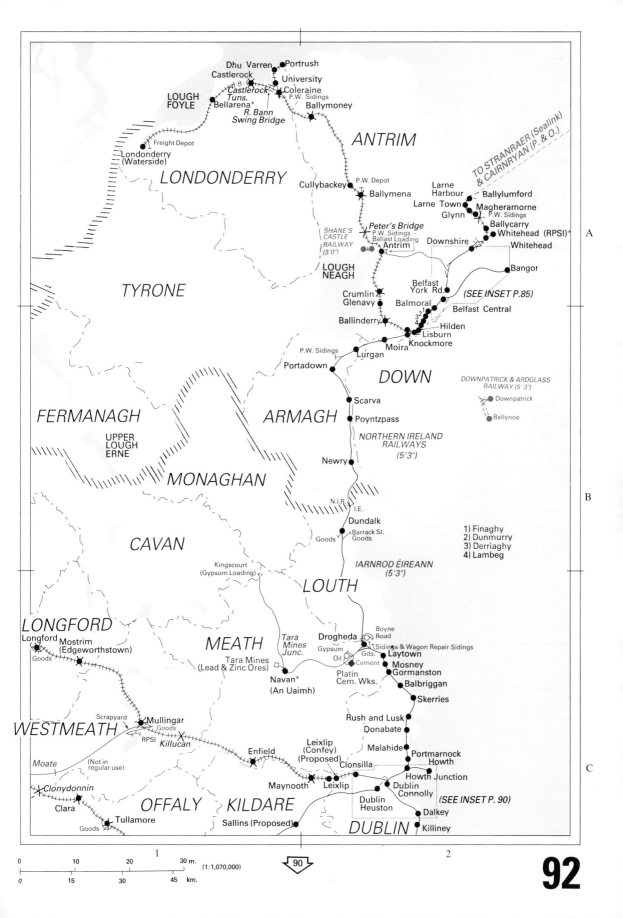

Dhu Varren ● ●Portrush
Castlerock ●University
Castlerock ✕ ●Coleraine
Castlerock
Tuns. ●P.W. Sidings
Bellarena* ●Ballymoney
R. Bann
Swing Bridge

LOUGH
FOYLE

ANTRIM

TO STRANRAER (Sealink)
& CAIRNRYAN (P. & O.)*

Freight Depot
● Londonderry
(Waterside)

LONDONDERRY

●Cullybackey   P.W. Depot
✕
●Ballymena

Larne
Harbour ● ●Ballylumford
Larne Town ● ●Magheramorne
Glynn ● ●P.W. Sidings
✕ ●Ballycarry
●Whitehead (RPSI)*   A
Downshire ✕
Whitehead

TYRONE

SHANE'S
CASTLE
RAILWAY
(3'0")

Peter's Bridge
P.W. Sidings ✕
Ballast Loading
Antrim

Downshire

LOUGH
NEAGH

●Bangor

(SEE INSET P.85)

Belfast
York Rd.
Balmoral ●Belfast Central
3·2·1
4

Crumlin ●
Glenavy ●
Ballinderry ●

Hilden
Lisburn
Knockmore
Moira

DOWN

DOWNPATRICK & ARDGLASS
RAILWAY (5' 3")
✕ ●Downpatrick

●Ballynoe

P.W. Sidings
●Lurgan
●Portadown

●Scarva

●Poyntzpass

ARMAGH

NORTHERN IRELAND
RAILWAYS
(5'3")

FERMANAGH

UPPER
LOUGH
ERNE

●Newry

B

MONAGHAN

N.I.R.
I.E.
●Dundalk
Goods ●Barrack St.
Goods

IARNROD ÉIREANN
(5'3")

1) Finaghy
2) Dunmurry
3) Derriaghy
4) Lambeg

CAVAN

Kingscourt
(Gypsum Loading)

LOUTH

LONGFORD

Longford ✕ ●Mostrim
(Edgeworthstown)
Goods

MEATH

Tara
Mines
Junc.

Boyne
Road
Drogheda ●
Sidings & Wagon Repair Sidings
Gypsum
Oil ●
Gds. ●Laytown
Cement ●Mosney
●Gormanston

Tara Mines
(Lead & Zinc Ores)

Navan*
(An Uaimh)

Platin
Cem. Wks.

●Balbriggan

●Skerries

WESTMEATH

Scrapyard
✕ ●Mullingar
Goods
RPSI
✕ Killucan

●Rush and Lusk

●Donabate

●Enfield

Leixlip
(Confey)
(Proposed)

●Malahide

●Portmarnock
Howth

C

Moate

(Not in
regular use)

Clonsilla

Howth Junction

✕ Clonydonnin
Clara

Maynooth
✕ ●Leixlip

Dublin
Connolly

(SEE INSET P. 90)

●Tullamore
Goods ✕

Sallins (Proposed) ●

Dublin
Heuston

DUBLIN

●Dalkey

OFFALY   KILDARE

●Killiney

0   10   20   30 m.
(1:1,070,000)
0   15   30   45 km.

1   ▽90   2

92

ELECTRIFICATION MAP

———	Overhead electrified lines 25kV, 50Hz ac.
– – –	Overhead electrification authorised.
———	3rd rail electrification 750 volts dc. (LUL is all 660 volts dc 4th rail and Manchester to Bury is 1,200 volts dc 3rd rail).
- - - -	3rd rail electrification authorised
· · · ·	Overhead electrified lines 1,500 volts dc (except where shown otherwise).
———	Non-electrified line.

All North London suburban lines are ac electrified except Woodgrange Park Junc to Gospel Oak and Carlton Road Juncs, Cricklewood to Acton Wells Junc, and Mitre Bridge Junc to Clapham Junc. Drayton Park to Moorgate, the Snow Hill Tunnel and Richmond-Willesden-Stratford-N. Woolwich are 3rd rail.

Stratford to Camden Junction is dual electrified.

All SR suburban lines are electrified except the Angerstein Wharf branch and the Factory Junction/Clapham Junction to Kensington line.

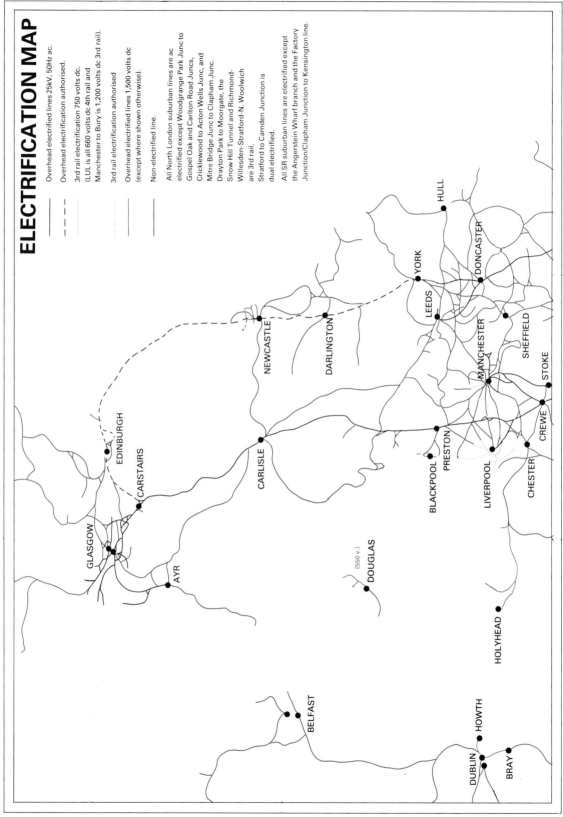

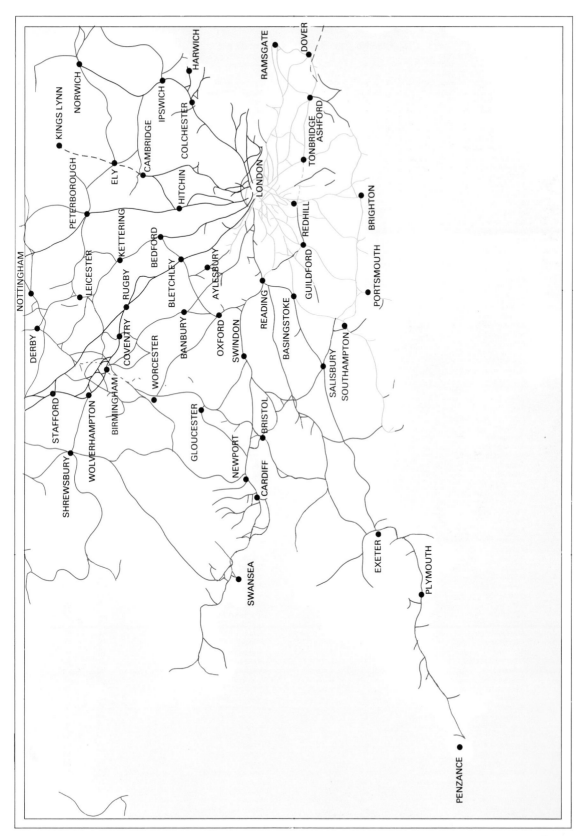

INDEX

All passenger stations are included in this index. Freight terminals, junctions, names, tunnels and other significant locations are indexed where their names or map references differ from an adjoining passenger station.

97

98

101

114

118

INDEX TO BRITISH RAIL LOCOMOTIVE STABLING POINTS, CARRIAGE DEPOTS & LOCOMOTIVE WORKS